MW00881981

AMERICA ON SUICIDE WATCH

THE RISE OF THE PROGRESSIVE SUPERSTATE AND THE FALL OF THE AMERICAN "IDEA"

RICHTER WATKINS

Copyright © 2016 Richter Watkins

All rights reserved.

Published in the United States by Poco Creek Publishing

Watkins, Richter. America On Suicide Watch. 1st ed.

An autopsy of history will show that all great nations eventually commit suicide.

–Arnold J. Toynbee

Dedicated to Indie and Kieran
with the hope that the core values
of this great nation will continue to exist
for their generation.

INTRODUCTION

Grassroots America feels it has lost its heritage and is being robbed of its future by elites who serve powerful interest groups and not the people who put them in power. And they see their country in serious decline. There is the spreading realization that America as a culture has lost the sense of personal responsibility, of civility, and is falling to massive debt and global weakness that can only lead to a disastrous end. There is a growing fear that America is rapidly on its way to becoming a failed state whose intelligentsia, media and entertainment industry play a major roll in the decline.

America is staring into the abyss and, as Nietzsche suggested, the abyss is staring back. The shovels that dig the graves of nations are massive debt, corrupt bureaucracies and a leadership in the throes of delusional visions. It's not the first time America faced destruction by its own misguided leaders.

The rebellion brewing isn't a simple election insurrection by the disgruntled. It is a deep and profound awakening. America is once again facing a major civil and constitutional conflict.

The very beginning of this nation was nearly stillborn at Plymouth Rock when a collectivist religious order failed 400 years ago. But after that near disaster they were saved by an amazing reversal of course and the birth of a new 'idea' that would end up being codified in the Constitution and Bill of Rights and lead to the greatest political experiment and success in history.

That great 'idea' of social, political and economic freedom is being seriously challenged once again by a renewed collectivist mindset. Socialist tribal collectivism keeps coming back, like the undead, just in different clothes.

Whether we can reverse course, as we have several times in the past, one thing is clear. Americans will not go quietly into the dark night.

The purpose of this book is to lay the groundwork, reveal the underlying conflict, and suggest the urgency of the battle ahead if we are to avoid the fate of those great nations who have failed to preserve their core values and committed suicide.

CONTENTS

ONE

AMERICA'S IDENTITY CRISIS

It has been our fate as a nation not to have ideologies, but to be one.

–Richard Hofstadter

IN NOVEMBER OF 1620, English Separatist leader William Bradford, determined to find greater freedom for his religion, crossed the stormy Atlantic on the hundred-foot Mayflower with 102 passengers and 60 crew.

After their amazing, treacherous journey the pilgrims landed at Plymouth Rock and set up shop in the wilderness of America and began the creation of one of the first uncontested, religious based, socialist experiments: from each according to his ability to each according to his need, far in advance of Marx, but with similar, disastrous results.

The experiment went on for almost two years.

Food, clothing and shelter were doled out from the common stores, everyone pitching in to keep the colony afloat. It didn't work. No one profited in the colony from working extra hard on inventing new ways and new tools. In a collective environment there is a built-in lack of incentive above the lowest common denominator.

The religious passion that motivated the experiment is that human beings would be more industrious and creative when incentivized by the altruistic values and ruled by a religious collective on behalf of the greater good, than as individuals driven by self-interest where their religious beliefs and their ruling body weren't the same. One is spiritual, the other political.

The belief that self-interest could be overcome by an altruistic governing structure, yet still allow individual freedom, inventiveness and the drives necessary in a dangerous and unknown wilderness, turned out to be a near fatal illusion. With their European and English background the pilgrims didn't have the survival techniques of indigenous tribes. To gain them they would have to toss out their own heritage, which they had no desire or ability to do.

Tribal communalism can only exist with iron rule and rigid obedience to low level survival tools as demonstrated everywhere it exists. Tribes cannot allow intellectual creativity, individualism, freedom to invent and innovate, and that is exactly what the

American wilderness demanded of these descendants of European history. They tried a religious collectivist vision and it failed.

In many respects, Europe's entire history is a struggle between the tyranny of tribalism and the liberation of individual intelligence. That conflict lay at the very heart of the Plymouth Rock pilgrims.

The tribal mind is static, backwards looking; it is uncreative and antagonistic to evolving. Tribes often last for thousands of years without developing any science, literature, or economic commercialism.

When advanced civilizations return to a collective stasis, as America is on course to accomplish, the consequences are inevitably disastrous.

The Plymouth Rock pilgrims didn't come from small, wilderness tribes adjusted to collective iron rule, they came from a major, complex civilization and the attempt to return to one-dimensional tribal rule, without the means by which such tribes survive was doomed from the start.

Mate selection, personal ego needs, territorial competiveness and other fundamental survival instincts cannot be erased by any form of altruistic collectivism, retraining camps, or powerful religiosity.

Given the sophistications of European history, the colonists weren't good candidates for wilderness tribalism.

BRADFORD'S COLONY DESCENDED into poverty, misery and disease from which all the communal prayers on earth couldn't save them. The result was the death of half the colony, including Bradford's beloved wife.

He secretly buried the dead so the indigenous people didn't see the colony in collapse, yet it was those same Native Americans, maybe much to their later dismay, who helped these early colonists survive. From that came our Thanksgiving.

The choice for the pilgrims was either to attempt to live as the Indians, an existence that for them would have been a Hobbesian one, nasty, brutish and short, or surrender to the reality that a radical reversal of the colony's communal philosophy was necessary.

The demands of survival and heritage forced Bradford after those first disastrous years of failure to hold a meeting in 1623 to deal with the problem. It ended with freeing his flock from the ruling chains of tribal religious communalism.

With that monumental decision, Bradford, who would later become a five-time governor of Massachusetts, became one of the progenitors of America's unique experiment.

If you want a better cabin, one with a stove, even a pump for running water, then invent and build it, and along the way, you may win the mate of your choice.

Thus, in death and defeat of the original

collectivist vision of what America should be, was born the beginnings of the 'idea' of what America could be.

William Bradford's voluminous writings about those struggles of 'Plymouth Plantation' would influence intellectuals in England, such as John Locke, who in turn would have a significant influence on the thinking of our Founding Fathers in what became the Golden Age of political thought.

This nation gave up early on the belief in rule by elites, and 'positive' governance, operating under the guise of altruistic collectivism. America turned against the concept that allowed rulers to do whatever they thought was right, just, or, more often than not, convenient.

The Founders created the base of this radical new form of grassroots self-rule in the Constitution and the Bill of Rights.

The new vision could best be described as 'negative' governance and would define the nation's inherit ideology as the sovereignty of the people.

This American experiment was despised around the globe by elitist rulers, but admired by the common people of those oppressive regimes.

Now, having forgotten her history, America is in the process of repeating the disaster of our beginning by creating a centralized command-and-control government in complete contradiction to the core values that made this nation history's freest, most powerful, and wealthiest republic.

The metastatic growth of Washington's power, its smothering weight, has triggered something the Pilgrims didn't have to deal with, a serious factional divide that foreshadows a potentially dangerous, revolutionary future.

We are in a classic struggle between proponents of progressive big government, and those who want to return to small government and the fundamental individualist values that made America the most powerful, innovative and wealthy nation on earth. This factionalism is what the Founding Fathers feared. We are now a house seriously divided.

TWO

THE UNMAKING OF AMERICA

A nation is either in the making or the unmaking.

–Jose Ortega Y Gasset, *The Revolt of the Masses*

THE FORCES OF A NATION'S UNMAKING begin with the radicalization of the intelligentsia and the wide appeal of a society run by an all-powerful, bureaucratic state that promises to fulfill the wants and needs of the people.

If the growing rebellion against the progressive Superstate fails, America will join those great empires and nations of the past who dug their graves by violating the principles that made them powerful in the first place.

The economic, political and moral foundation of America is under attack. The Founders knew that a republic could not long exist without strong families and communities under the affirmation of civic virtues and personal responsibility that enable limited government and universal freedoms to exist.

The alternative is some form of tyranny, a condition where one bows to authority and is told how to live and what to think.

The rise of political correctness, where our very essence as a constitutional republic is under attack by a radical left intelligentsia, is succeeding in its ambition to bring the nation down off its high horse.

All cultures are now considered equal in this multicultural era. Those traditional Americans who refuse to accept America's demotion are diminished by the progressive secular religion in power.

As the nation weakens across the globe, her military cut in half, her debt doubled, and her principle enemies strengthened, we may face a clash of civilizations for which we will be utterly unprepared. If the rebellious spirit of America isn't yet dead in this warp speed, dangerous world, it is in serious trouble.

When the slumbering millennials, the largest generation in our history, finally awaken they will have to make critical decisions that will determine their lives and the nation's future. They will either finish pounding the final nails in the coffin of our constitutional governance, and learn the art of bowing before the master class, or they will rebel and force a reversal of America's course as William Bradford did.

AMERICA'S PROGRESSIVE ASSAULT on our core values is driven by an ideology whose vision is a complete transformation of this nation into a government run tribal collective.

The Obama administration, supported by the media and university cognoscenti, sought from the beginning to overturn the old order and build their vision of a new order. They promised to end the wars in the Middle East, reduce our military footprint, put rational environmental controls on our climate killing, disaster-capitalism, and end the horror of 'white privilege'.

But overturning America might not prove as easy a task as first assumed. The nation was built on a revolutionary idea unique in history: that individual rights and freedoms exist before, and without the consent of, or subservience to, the 'State'. That is, individuals have fundamental sovereignty.

There is a mounting grassroots rebellion driven by the realization that the ideology at the nation's core, its DNA, is once again seriously threatened.

The highly stressed middle class knows they have no representation, they are the sacrificial lambs to the gigantic appetite of the federal government's massive, incompetent overreach.

The rising 'outsider' rebels see the progressive left's ambitions as a sophomoric, delusional fantasy. But they also realize that if the radical transformation isn't stopped, if America's decline reaches a tipping point, there might be no chance of a reversal of our disastrous course.

America, the radical left contends, is the dark source of the world's ills. Its economic capitalist system created climate change that is behind the rise of radical Islamist jihad, and most of the other miseries around the globe. The radical left makes no excuses for its hatred of traditional America and its economic system.

The origin of the current 'unmaking' of America that brought Barack Obama to office begins with an understanding of the rise of the modern progressive left and how, from the muck and corruption of Chicago, they reached the seat of the world's greatest power.

THREE

The Progressive Revolution

. . . all totalitarian movements are an attempt
to return to tribalism.
That, in the end, is what this great internal battle is all about.

–Karl R. Popper, *The Open Society and its Enemies*

THE TOTALITARIAN MOVEMENTS of the last century that Popper referred to grew out of an ideology that is far from dead—socialism. Like the undead, this tribal ideology keeps coming back in new clothes.

The latest version isn't about the state directly taking over the means of production, it's about controlling the means of production by directing the flow of economic energy as the rulers see fit for goals *they* determine.

The cognoscenti are excited by what they see as

the great synthesis, that combining of capitalism and socialism, with the socialist element on top, of course. It is the foundation of the progressives of our time.

When, as Popper suggested, the state becomes the highest moral authority in the land, liberty will not prevail.

China is the supreme model with its capitalistic zones and its socialist government using the production of those zones for whatever purposes the rulers determine.

STATE CONTROLLED CAPITALISM is where the State replaces the middle class as the dominant market force. This pushes the dwindling middle class down Hayek's well-travelled, *Road to Serfdom'*.

The transition of progressive thought to its current manifestation, far more radical than was the case with Presidents Woodrow Wilson or Franklin Roosevelt, emerged from the violent rebellion in the 60s against LBJ's disastrous war in Vietnam and his hated draft. The takeover of the progressive movement by neo-Marxists like Saul Alinsky gave the radicals a view that wasn't evolutionary, it was revolutionary.

The progressives adamantly deny the narrative of America's heroic Founding Fathers. It's really, they argue, about a bunch of privileged rich 'white' guys like George Washington who wanted to keep all their wealth out of the hands of the English coffers. Patriotism is nothing but a sham.

This is the catechism preached across the universities.

As Lincoln suggested, the philosophy of the schoolroom becomes the philosophy of government in the next generation. We're experiencing that truth.

THE TRADITIONAL NARRATIVE insists government's function isn't to lead the people to nirvana, religious obeisance, paradise, or royal submission, but rather to restrain those tyrannical ambitions.

The great fear of constitutional conservatives is that, unless there is, as happened with Bradford, a major course correction, the American 'idea' will be destroyed by the combination of dependency, broken family structure, massive debt, irrational statist controls, and irreconcilable factions.

The traditional vision is that pursuit of happiness was your business, your challenge, not some 'leader' or worse yet, some distant bureaucratic blockhead.

Many Republican elites believed for a long time that their view was self-evident, so they weren't inspired to fight for Main Street against the forces that are radically changing America. Their impotence has unleashed the rise of the 'outsiders' triggering a rebellion against the Washington Beltway.

THE FOUNDERS FEARED that generations would eventually emerge who would undo everything that the nation stood for on the basis of a radical political vision that would preach a catechism of State Supremacy.

Those much feared generations have arrived and they are undoing the American foundation at an amazing rate and with little consequential opposition . . . until now.   A great awakening of the much maligned middle class has triggered the rise of the growing insurgency against the establishment.

If America's success is based on having encoded private property, encouraging productive ambition on free markets, and the foundation supported by the inculcation of moral responsibility, those concepts are under fire.

The concepts that created the power of America weren't accepted in Central and South American countries, resulting in their remaining impoverished Third World banana republics for hundreds of years.

Venezuela, with its bountiful resources and industrious people, was believed by many observers to overtake America over a century ago. But instead of copying the economic and political ideology of capitalism, that country, under leaders like Hugo Chavez, turned to socialism and slid into abject poverty.

THE ANTI-AMERICAN MENTALITY in our universities, encouraged by the literati and progressive politicians, insists we are a nation of 'Indian' killers, slavers, climate destroyers and hegemonic war mongers. They believe that nothing in our history is meritorious.

The traditional view, on the contrary, insists it was that the superior economic engine of the North that defeated the South's plantation economy and freed the slaves.

The South's cotton economy was no match for the factories, machines, rails and weapon production of the North despite the South's dedicated soldiers, and superior generals. The power of capitalism as the primary force in the victory over the South is no longer the dominant narrative. That narrative has changed. That great victory is attributed to the emancipation proclamation that freed the slaves allowing them to join the fight. Capitalism is an irrelevant issue.

A mere seven years after the brutal Civil War that cost 750,000 lives and devastated entire cities, America rose to become, and remains to this day, the greatest productive machine and liberator of mankind from oppression and poverty that the world has ever seen.

Less than a hundred years after the devastations of the Civil War the battle against the Axis powers of Nazi Germany, Italy and Japan, had the same result for the same reason that the North prevailed over the South—American capitalism. It was the engine that supplied all the allies, including the impoverished, totalitarian Soviet Union, with the munitions, tanks and planes needed in battle.

Yet the socialists of that era, those weavers of subjective fantasies and big lies, gave the victory to the Soviets.

Another ongoing issue is the jealousy intellectuals have toward the market economy where the big rewards go to the most productive entrepreneurs, tinkerers, inventors and not to the gold-star cognoscenti.

The modern progressive's disdain for free market capitalism has many fathers, the most important being Marx and his historic offspring, the neo-Marxists.

Few have stated the idea of anti-capitalism much more forcefully than the socialist German leader in a speech in 1927, "We are socialist, we are enemies of today's capitalistic economic system for the exploitation of the economically weak, with its unfair salaries, with its unseemly evaluation of a human being according to wealth and property instead of responsibility and performance, and we are all determined to destroy this system under all conditions."

Thus spoke the great anti-capitalist, warrior, tribal socialist leader himself, German Chancellor Adolf Hitler. And he knew who to scapegoat and mass murder—those Jews who'd become so successful on the commercial market and banking.

THE TRIBAL COLLECTIVIST MOVEMENTS of the last century, whether socialist, its fascist offshoot, or communist, all agreed that free market capitalism must be destroyed. That has been modified. The democratic welfare state is the new model.

While success in the post WWII period in building quasi-socialist welfare regimes seemed to work for a time in Europe and England, nations that were saved by capitalist America who assisted not only their rebuilding, but for more than a half century, their protection, now are beginning to weaken. Greece collapsed under debt only to be temporarily saved by Germany. France is in near financial collapse as well. It's just the beginning.

If Europe again falls, it is doubtful America will have the power to pick up the pieces.

The Fifties Eisenhower restraint freeze-framed American postwar culture and the nation fell behind the European Welfare States bureaucratization of society.

The end of the conservative Eisenhower era was followed by a brief libertarian phase that began with the election of John Kennedy. The young were demanding more social freedoms and JFK seemed the right man for the time. He lowered the taxes that

Eisenhower had raised to pay down the war debt. Kennedy encouraged the recognition and integration of the black community, and demanded that the Democratic Party, the party of racism and Jim Crow, leave that dark past behind and embrace the future.

JFK'S ASSASSINATION changed everything. It elevated to power the most progressive man since FDR, Lyndon Johnson, a dark operator in political chess in the senate and congress. But his beltway brilliance would have terrible consequences outside of those hallowed halls. His Great Society programs would have long-term disastrous effects on the inner cities, and his war in Vietnam would create the radical forces that now are in power.

All radical movements need major trigger points to gain traction in a society, especially one like America. Vietnam would be that trigger point and lead to the protest movement in the hands of radical neo-Marxists like Saul Alinsky, a community organizer in Chicago well before Obama.

The streets in the 60s and early 70s were filled with radicals running around with Mao's *Little Red Book* as a badge of honor, ignoring the reality that Mao was one of the greatest mass murderers in history, or justifying those murders as necessary to rid that country of an even greater evil—capitalism.

The sex, drugs and rock-n-roll generation was

taken over by neo-Marxist radicals joined by the Black Panthers, the SDS, the Port Heron Statement, and the violent bombers of the Weather Underground. Chicago became one of the major epicenters for this radicalism and would remain so.

But this radical movement would be forced largely underground through the Nixon, Bush, Reagan, and Clinton years.

THE RADICAL LEFT'S AMBITIONS desperately needed exploitable crises if they were to have any chance of a resurrection. Those crises arrived in post 9/11 with G. W. Bush's war in Iraq and the housing bust that created a major recession. It was a perfect combination.

The left went after the Bush/Cheney regime with all the fury of a full-on Saul Alinsky 'Rules for Radicals' character assassination and the road to power suddenly opened as an exhausted nation was looking for some major change.

But the one thing missing was a great political leader to carry out the mission of tearing down old America and bringing forth a leftist transformation. And where else would he come from but Chicago.

Barack Obama was the radical progressive's dream come true. A charismatic speaker, former community organizer, heir to Alinsky, and fully dedicated to fulfilling the neo-Marxist's ambition of undoing the myth of America. Obama also carried that all-powerful weapon, the redemptive race card.

Now the left would become the 'man' and have the power and mission to transform evil America. The dream that arose in the rebellious 60s finally reached the seat of the world's great superpower with the intent of revolutionary transformation of 'white privileged' capitalist America.

FOUR

THE SECOND COMING

The ceremony of innocence is drowned;
The best lack all conviction, while the worst
Are full of passionate intensity.
Surely some revelation is at hand;
Surely the Second Coming is at hand.

–W. B. Yeats, *The Second Coming*

CANDIDATE BARACK OBAMA articulated with flare and high drama what he and his devoted followers passionately believed: "We are the ones we've been waiting for. We are the change that we seek."

He was met with wild, resounding applause by the radical left. It was just the beginning of the pied piper's radical progressive takeover of the Democratic Party and America.

Obama fed the starving souls of old Boomer

leftists and a new legion of progressive true believers. All things suddenly seem possible, dreams coming true. Imagine the new world of your subjective desires and then go out and get the power to bring it into being as an objective reality.

Joy returned to long depressed radicals. There was light at the end of the tunnel, a leader who could guide them to the Promised Land, their manifest destiny. Or, critics feared, their manifest fantasy.

It wasn't a political movement so much as a religious passion masquerading as politics. Its fundamental premise was the radical change of reviled America. Down with idiotic patriotism and up with political correctness as defined by progressive transformational ideology.

The ascent to the throne of the anti-Bush under the flag of 'hope and change' sent shock waves of excitement and joy also across the wider liberal landscape not seen since JFK. This first 'black' Camelot hero streaked across the political sky of leftist fantasy like a historic, brilliant meteor. He landed in their hearts and minds, setting their dreams aflame.

His rise to power was accompanied by the heart-throbbing drumbeat of a new crusade that would surely roll back the oceans and bring a new light to the darkness of America's soul, while resetting our relationship with a world we'd so long aggrieved.

The crusading Obamanistas marched forth out of

the dark, corrupt, political muck of Chicago, hitting the streets of America and the world stage with a sense of historic ambition. They were met, not with the skepticism that any politicians from Chicago normally warrant, but with resounding applause from sea-to-shining-sea.

Not to be left behind, the literati, media and Hollywood elite jumped on board the grand celebration. These social elites that Lenin referred to as, "the commanding heights of the culture."

The African/American savior of the nation's racist soul had arrived to carry out our redemption. Finally and forever, the victorious radicals proclaimed, America would shed the evil of the nation's horrible past and a new, inclusive, peace-loving, multicultural social justice Camelot would emerge.

We would finally be loved, admired and accepted around the cheering globe amid a veritable floatation of soft stellar music and beautiful gardens of flowers, not guns, oil or stinking capitalist greed. America would be embraced, hugged, and join the community of nations not as their superior, but as their equal.

The beautiful hope-and-change vision of the progressive champion took believers to their knees, tears glistened in their overjoyed eyes. The political religiosity that surged forth had such power that once supposedly objective journalists surrendered to the emotional subjective worship, casting aside normal skepticism, reason and objectivity. Their political god had dropped from progressive heaven and they swooned with unabashed surrender.

OBAMA TOOK THE REINS OF POWER unchained by America's evil corrupting capitalist influences: like ever having had a real job, made or sold consumer products, or become despoiled by the malevolent world of Wall Street.

He was a diamond in the rough waiting to be polished by the greatness of the transformative legacy actions he promised once in the White House.

When he ascended to the throne, he had House and Senate in his hands. He articulated his agenda to great applause: to end poverty, racist inequality, and fossil fuel gluttony by putting tight reins on rampant, disaster capitalism run by the greatest of evils—'white privilege'. His social justice welfare state would exceed anything being tried on earth. He was creating a Superstate for the sake of the greater good.

His charismatic style, stellar message and luminous smile dropped Hollywood, the liberal media, and leftist literati to their knees like parishioners in an impassioned church, like young girls screaming before a new boy's band.

Obama's ascension hit media stars hard, like MSNBC's Chris Mathews who said he felt a thrill up his leg, and he was not alone. Obama had political sex appeal the left couldn't resist. Much of that thrill would vanish later, but in the beginning hope-and-change it was so, so exciting. Thrills went up many legs.

So began this transformational pied piper's historic journey of redemption and revival. His disciples bowed before him and all he needed to achieve success was a firm grip on political reality here and abroad, a grip he would prove, tragically, not to have.

Obama's ideology was grounded in glowing stellar concepts, not earthly political precepts. His fantasy world was a brilliant bubble that flew well above the hard, cold realities of the world below.

JUST WHO THIS REDEMPTIVE PRESIDENT really was hadn't been asked by voters or the pundits, but would be now that he'd reached the pinnacle of power. What values would he bring into the seat of the world's great superpower that would ultimately determine the success or failure of his administration here and on the world stage? The answer would turn out to be very complex in origin.

Peter Beinart, author of 'The Crisis of Zionism', stated that Obama took office, "with a distinctly progressive vision of Jewish identity. . . ." And Obama would label himself as the first Jewish president. Many conservative Jews weren't so enthusiastic about that self-identity.

Other powerful influences that formed pieces of the puzzle of Obama's complex mindset were his living in Islamic Indonesia, and his abandonment by his parents, a leftist white mother and a radical anti-colonial Kenyan father.

Then came his major radical political influences: Weather Underground leader and bomber Bill Ayers, America-hating historian Howard Zinn, leftist professors at Colombia and Harvard. And, of course, Obama's religious mentor over the years, Chicago's infamous America hating, Grace Baptist Church minister, Jeremiah *'Goddamn America'* Wright.

Last but not least, the powerful influence, maybe the most powerful of all, was Obama's ideologically impregnation by Chicago's anti-Vietnam War radicals, devoted disciples of neo-Marxist community organizer, Saul Alinsky. This neo-Marxist created the political weapons still being widely used by the radical left to this day.

Long after the radical master's death in 1972, Alinsky's *'Rules for Radicals'* would remain a powerful operational bible for radicals and his two devoted disciples were Barack Obama and Hillary Clinton.

Alinsky considered 'ridicule' to be the most potent weapon in the attack arsenal as it undermined rational discussion, turning everything emotional, and made logic and facts irrelevant. It is the prevalent standard used across the political correct campuses, in the campaigns against Republicans and conservative oppositions. It is used nonstop in the shaming of Main Street America. Reason gives way to ridicule, conversation gives way to condemnation.

If you are defined as evil by the left, that is you're not under the 'spell' of the 'vision', then all the arguments in the world mean absolutely nothing. You must be kept out of the circle of discussion. You don't count. You're the enemy and must be ridiculed into irrelevancy.

Even worse, if you're a black conservative you're a traitor, a disgusting Uncle Tom and have no rights on any stage. Leftist Chicago politicos like Rahm Emanuel nurtured the young Obama for high office, knowing from the start they had a winner. Obama was not only going to be the first African/American president, but the most progressive in history.

It didn't matter that Obama actually had no lineage to the past of American slavery. What mattered was that he had no negatives in his background. He had been, like Alinsky, a community organizer. With a Kenyan father and white mother, he was black enough, and he had a brilliant rhetorical gift in reading his team's well-crafted speeches. He had been educated in the esteemed Ivy League and was a senator from Illinois. All in all, Obama brought a very powerful resume to the progressive stable.

Race and ridicule were the two great weapons that progressives and their media henchmen would use to run Hillary Clinton out of town and win Barack

Obama two terms against soft, reach-across-the-isle, establishment conservative opponents.

The greatest of weapons Obama brought in his campaign to transform and downgrade hegemonic America was that of divide and conquer. All the major forces on the right had to be relentlessly attacked. They were charged with causing terrible wars, maintaining structural racism, being sexist and anti-Islamic. The police were out of control killers of innocent blacks. And the worst were the evil capitalists who were destroying the climate which in turn created the Islamic jihad and ISIS.

Thus, Obama could announce to the enemy his timetable for pulling out of Afghanistan and Iraq, ending our wars long before the enemy was ready to surrender. His declaration of peace to the world surely would calm our enemies down.

It reminded many of that famous line of Trotsky's, "You may not want war, but war may want you."

EUROPEAN LIBERALS were so thrilled to see the ascent of this progressive 'black' American president that they fell instantly in mad love. He was awarded the Nobel Peace Prize before he launched his first drone strike.

Obama's insult to Churchill when he removed the great man's bust from the White House and unceremoniously sent it back to London in a tribute to his anti-colonial, Kenyan father, was not seen as an insult by the progressive establishment in England, but rather a tribute to modern PC sensitivity.

The radical forces came to power armed with certainty of their cause. Failure wasn't possible as they were, after all, the best and brightest, the gold-star students. Obama assured the Europeans that peace and global tranquility were on the way. And he would guide the forces of good to clean up the global environment. His legacies would be extraordinary. He fully intended to go down in history as one of our greatest presidents, if not *the* greatest.

And Obama had the tools to accomplish his goals. Both the House and Senate were in his hands, the media, Hollywood, university literati and late night TV. He couldn't fail once he got the rightwing pushed back into the woods where they belonged. And if they were resistant, Obama had the IRS and other agencies to deal with them.

MEANWHILE, THE SLUMBERING MILLENNIALS who were born in the Reagan era, grew up under the Clinton and Bush regimes, bore witness to the passionate religification of politics, fell for the rapture of hope-and-change, and convinced all was well, snuggled back into their pillow-soft lives, wishing to awake only at Spring Break, or the next Apple release. They had no idea how rude would be their awakening.

FIVE

The Dimming Light on the Hill

Look back over the past, with its changing
empires that rose and fell,
and you can foresee the future, too.

–Marcus Aurelius

THE MUGGING OF AMERICA'S SELF-IMAGE by the Obama administration's hostile view of this nation is widely accepted in America's universities and literati. It insists we are not, and never were, civilization's beacon.

Therefore the only acceptable solution is to reduce the power and arrogant patriotism of the republic by ending the whole concept of America's proclaimed exceptionalism. That, Obama made clear, would be the keystone of his legacy.

He's been remarkably successful.

The dazed establishment Republicans stood spellbound on the sidelines with grim political resignation, waiting to see what horrors were coming forth from the dark den of Chicago's corruption and fakery. They seemed shocked at how the people could become so deluded. It was almost as if the Republicans had been living so long in their own country-club bubble they'd also lost contact with the grassroots.

What made it even more painful was the absence of a charismatic Reaganesque alternative anywhere on the horizon to save the nation from what the conservatives feared was about to destroy the republic they loved, yet hadn't well defended. For them it was like being in a gunfight at high noon on Main Street and realizing their guns had no bullets.

The radical left had been told by Saul Alinsky to study and learn from the great Chicago gangster, Al Capone. The gangster had great talent in gaining power and destroying enemies.

They did, but in the end they underestimated the underlying DNA of grassroots Americans, just as they would underestimate America's global enemies.

The Republican establishment seemed utterly confused and lost when the outsider rebellion became a serious challenger.

Swollen with massive debt and a weakening global presence, this radically changed nation casts a grim shadow over that shining light on the hill, threatening to extinguish it altogether. It is a future the millennials will inherit, but not one they would be happy with.

The progressive attack on America is that we aren't an exceptional nation, but rather one of massive crimes against humanity and mother earth. This attack has been very successful and has engendered major self-doubt and doubt is a significant weapon in the hands of those seeking dominance for the sake of creating some vision of a collectivist welfare Superstate that violates everything America once stood for.

If America was the ideological birth of true freedom, its glorious run as the world's freest, most powerful nation is being savaged and brought to ruin from within by a successful progressive assault, and a feckless response by the Republican establishment.

THE RADICAL TRANSFORMATION OF AMERICA to a modern form of communal collectivism ruled from Washington, powered by technology, and driven by a gospel of multiculturalism, diversity, open borders and environmentalism, demands complete bureaucratization of the nation, and the end of our core 'idea' that set us apart.

You are an enemy of the new order if you resist the politically correct revolution and continue with your wrongful thinking. You are an ego-driven materialist in your personal pursuits, rather than becoming altruistic minded, 'degrowther' collectivist. And that means you must change or be ridiculed into extinction.

In the most fundamental sense, America is either a nation operating on the theory of 'positive' *big* governance, or one run on the theory of restricted 'negative' *small* governance.

So extreme is the factional ideological divide that it portends a nasty, potentially violent struggle looming in the near future. Unlike the old Democratic Party, the radicals in power came from the legacy of street action. Unlike the old Republican Party, the emergent Heartland 'insurgency' wasn't ready to surrender to the new era. They wanted their constitutional republic and its market economy back.

James Madison suggested that factions would eventually strangle freedom and destroy the republic. By dividing the nation up in antagonistic 'grievance' groups, Obama has set the stage of Madison's fear.

If America is to survive as a dynamic, exceptional, free society it must find a way to reassert its fundamental ideology. The nation that originated in the Enlightenment and evolved from the Renaissance and Reformation with the help of thinkers like Montesquieu, John Locke, Francis Bacon, and Descartes, and others of the Age of Reason, is once again being seriously challenged. What is at the heart of the struggle is the freedom of the individual.

THE IDEA OF THE SOVEREIGN INDIVIDUAL arrived after a long, painful development, coming to fruition in America not as a member of a tribe, a serf, peasant or cog, but as an individual with absolute, fundamental rights beyond the clutches of any tribe, royal government, or church authority.

This unique 'idea' of sovereignty of the individual that came to rule in America is under an all-out attack.

As author Mark Steyn put it, "An America that abandons the American idea will be a turbulent society." That may well be something of an understatement.

America created the most radical revolution in political history of what a person's value should be. This nation was built on the rejection of centralized power, opting instead for the value of freedom and individualism.

The Republican establishment was apoplectic when the radical progressives came to power, viewing the Obamanistas as a gathering of young, hungry vampires preparing to suck the blood from every lucrative artery in the country, to feed their gluttonous ambitions as the quasi-socialist governments in Europe were doing.

But when Republicans won the House and Senate, the anticipated changes didn't happen. Nothing changed. Anger grew across the Heartland at this utterly inept, go-along, get along political weakness in the establishment. While the progressive left charged ahead, the beltway Republican opposition limped behind, eating their dust.

The shocked and disturbed middle class of America, having lost income, jobs and faith in their country, knowing that they, not ISIS, were the real enemy of the progressive left, that they were the ones with targets on their back, had no real defenders in Washington fighting for them.

They needed a voice, a Howard Beale rage, "I'M MAD AS HELL, AND I'M NOT GOING TO TAKE THIS ANYMORE!"

That voice trumpeted back in 2009, and lit a small fire that spread across Main Street America.

SIX

A HEARTLAND INSURGENCY RISES

Man is free if he needs to obey no person, but solely the laws.

–Immanuel Kant

THE POPULIST MOVEMENT that grew out of the frustrations and disenfranchisement of grassroots America has become a serious force that now divides the Republican party and this nation in critical ways that resemble the big conflicts of our history. We appear to be heading for a major political and constitutional showdown that threatens the very definition of who we are. This is a revolutionary period, the house is radically divided and it threatens the uniqueness, the core 'idea' that created America.

What Europe didn't have, and what the new world offered was a place to put ideas into play without all the roadblocks and political and social barriers entrenched in the old world. America was invented, as it were, from whole cloth.

Since America's beginning, there has always been a deep philosophical hostility to powerful centralized government and the rule of elites.

The Founding Fathers wanted the separation of the individual, family and community from the national government in ways never tried before. This society grew rapidly from the ground up, from the small community to the larger collection of communities with the ambition, through the republic and constitution, to restrain federal power and keep freedom.

The values of early America, formed by the struggles in the wilderness that created endless challenges in organization, invention, risk and reward, was an adventure socially and politically unlike any other place on earth.

We were built literally by trial and error, challenge and response, giving birth to the unique and exceptional 'idea' of individual and community living in a freedom unknown anywhere in the world.

European royalty and intelligentsia never thought America's collection of state entities and territories, plus the big issue of slavery in the South, could possibly be held together without a powerful central command government. They would be proven wrong.

As Charles Murray observed in his book *'American Exceptionalism'*, "America's secular nongovernmental activism in promoting education, cultural resources, assistance to the poor, and social justice from the Founding onward has no counterpart in history of any other nation."

Given this radical beginning America has always been an anomaly, an exception to the normal 'laws' of governance. The very idea of government deemed the servant, and not the master of the people was a shock felt across the political globe. It was a violation of history, radical and dangerously anti-tribal.

THE SOVEREIGNTY OF THE PEOPLE had no meaning to the world's political elites, nor to the radical progressives of the present whose political philosophy demands centralized power *'over'* the people, downsizing the individual in favor of a collective ideology, whether religious, secular progressive, socialist, or a straight forward predatory dictatorship.

The federal government has expanded to unprecedented size and now employs over 4.1 million people in 645 agencies. The Washington Beltway is now surrounded by the six richest counties in the country.

America is no longer a small government nation. Citizens now live under the weight and overreach of an incompetent, bloated, bureaucratization that reaches into every aspect of every person's life, insulting the very nature of this republic.

America that once was is disappearing. The formerly free republic is now run by corrupt politicians, their lobbyist donors and crony capitalists seeking advantages without having to fight on the open market and becoming richer and more separated from Main Street than ever before. The nation is a growing tyranny out of touch with the people they are supposed to serve.

The statistics across the nation are stunning. With 95 million people no longer looking for work, another 45 million on food stamps, the middle class has flat-lined, while the central government is vastly bigger and richer than anything in our history, we have different America, a bureaucratic Superstate.

THE SUPERSTATE ROSE TO POWER on the back of crises exploited by ideologues seeking the endless reach of power. It arrived with a well stated intention to put an end to our faux 'exceptionalism.' Crisis advances power. Power for the progressive is the means by which they seek to implement their vision. Crisis is critical for revolutionaries of any persuasion.

Climate change is a good example. It's a complex problem that demands major societies move out of third world production and into more sophisticated technologies. The United States gets cleaner all the time, while China, India and Iran's capital of Tehran are smog swamps.

But for progressives, climate change is the political gift that keeps on giving. That incompetent bureaucratic masterminds have a clue as to how to deal with the climate is a joke.

If anything can fight climate change, it will come from the great polluter nations rising out of their poverty, and the free markets figuring out alternatives fuels and cleaner global living as is increasingly being demanded by the people living in smog swamps. If, that is, they have a voice.

Great nations may seem to collapse overnight, but their leap into the political abyss is always preceded by generations that destroy the core values of their society, the values that produced the greatness in the first place.

Nations may evolve and change, but they still must maintain the central core of their strength. Once that is gone, the soul of the nation is dead. In our warp speed world, powerful nations fall more quickly than in the past.

A nation sinking in massive debt, dumbed down by the excessive weight of bureaucratization, with a mountain of unfunded liabilities and unpaid bills, is marching toward a destiny it will not like.

THE GRASSROOTS REBELLION growing on

Main Street is drawing in disaffected millennials, independents, and libertarians who are joining the constitutional conservative base in opposition to this new, master planned altruistic Superstate. But this resistance needed a voice and a message.

A message of discontent did sound early in Obama's first term, but it took time to grow and become a serious force.

The angry, much ridiculed fly-over folks, schooled in the old principles and values of the constitutional republic—freedom, family, community and church—no longer believe these values mean anything to the leaders on either side of the isle. They believe they are leaderless in Washington and without national recognition for the first time in American history.

These regular, grassroots folks desperately wanted to hear the call of a rebel who could fire a shot across the bow of Washington madness, who could raise the flag of a powerful principle around which to form a resistance, a rebellion in the powerful American tradition.

The first *I'M MAD AS HELL'* rant came not by some preacher, politician or TV broadcaster, but rather, in grand historic irony, from Wall Street.

Business reporter Rick Santelli decried early and loudly in 2009 that the direction of government's intrusion into the market demanded a response, something on the order of the *tea-into-the-sea* rejoinder, as was the case against England that helped trigger a revolution.

Santelli, whether he liked it or not, with a few words uttered in Howard Beale rage, lit a fire in the Heartland that would spread and burn hot in the hearts and minds of those ignored, denied, and reduced to a small people of no consequence.

THUS WAS BORN THE INFAMOUS TEA PARTY that quickly became the most maligned, mocked and attacked political movement of our time. It started small and seemed for a time little more than the last gasp of a pathetic remnant from the dead past.

But this despised grassroots movement didn't die off quickly, as was assumed. Its flames grew. The Tea Party went after state governor races and congressional seats.

Alarmed, the progressives went after the Tea Party in every way it could, from the IRS attacks to endless derisions and mockery. It was described as a quasi-fascist evil, so low on the political totem pole that it found few allies even in the Republican hierarchy and that would come back to haunt them.

What the Tea Party had, what kept them going against all odds, was the historic American political DNA, that fundamental political 'idea' that demanded government fear the people and not the other way around. An idea utterly incomprehensible to progressives because it suggested this malignancy wanted to put power back in the hands of the 'stupid' flyover folks.

The Tea Party was too insulting to be taken seriously, until it had to be. For powerful, prideful and privileged progressives, and many establishment Republicans, the Tea Party stopped being a pathetic fun piñata to bash. It became a serious enemy, and maybe just the tip of the spear of discontent.

The insurgency frightened establishment elites as the rebels seemed to possess some dangerous fundamental, seemingly unshakeable conviction in the traditional 'idea' of America. Suddenly those who thought the battle was over, that big government had won, now faced the shocking realization that the battle was just getting started.

IN THE LONG TRADITION OF AMERICA with its history of grassroots activism, these insurgents believed, as did their forebears, that the great catastrophes throughout history have been the bloody gift of some misguided, power-driven politicos determined to build their version of nirvana.

Traditional Americans have always rejected centralized power and the overreach of regulations, as well as charismatic government crusades, and the collectivization of society.

The radical left flank of the progressive

movement, not to be outdone, resurrected the long dead philosophy of socialism. It has once against risen from the dead, led this time by curmudgeon zombie warrior Bernie 'the burn' Sanders.

The factional divide in the world's most powerful nation is reaching a critical juncture. What is at stake, what lies at the very heart of the battle in this insurgent America, is that of losing the greatest principle of freedom, the sovereignty of the people.

SEVEN

WE THE PEOPLE

Any discussion of the political laws of the United States must always begin with the dogma of the sovereignty of the people.

–Alexis De Tocqueville, *Democracy in America*

WHILE MOST AMERICANS SLEPT the thieves of freedom stole their sovereignty one executive order and one pile of new regulations at a time, like political burglars in the night. Would there be an awakening? Will Americans, feeling the onerous weight of government smothering their ambitions and dreams, rebel? And what direction will that rebellion take?

The progressives behind America's transformation were aided and abetted for years by an impotent Republican establishment's lame response to the growing challenge.

The government's massive regulatory intrusion is a reversal of roles between the rulers and the ruled.

This was never seriously challenged by Republican 'insiders', which gave rise to the 'outsider' insurgency and the growing belief that the 'conservative' mantra of the 'insiders' was a fat cover for their ballooning perks, privileges and personal power.

IT IS NECESSARY, THE PROGRESSIVE INSISTS, that America reduce the sovereignty of the people into bureaucratic irrelevance in order for the new order to fully emerge.

This new order emerged in Europe and England as a widely assumed correction to the bloody disasters of last century's socialism, communism, and fascism. This correction being the hybrid Welfare State that is seen as a political Hegelian synthesis with capitalist zones making the wealth, but ruled and regulated by social justice administrators from on high.

If the great synthesis fails, as it appears to be doing from Greece to France and even now in China, the world may be in for a very nasty ride.

Barack Obama is a supreme believer in imposing this new order, this social justice welfare Superstate making government responsible for all things. In the all-powerful subjective mind of the modern progressive, government is the creator of the objective political and economic world, the director of all meaningful ecologies, the end all and be all of social existence. Those who stand in the way and don't want to cooperate are the enemy.

This hybrid political structure built on this new 'command and control' philosophy is, in a sense, the last best hope for something positive to come out of elitist Statism. The new model, replacing the disaster of the Soviet Union, is China.

CHINA'S RISE FROM THE DEPTHS OF POVERTY and misery, following the mass-murder regime of Mao, went forward in the post-Mao era, creating 'big push industrialization' under men like Deng Xiaoping. Yet China maintained totalitarian control and lack of democracy except within the confines of the party. They sought productivity, not democracy. Their system is technically closer to a form of fascism than socialism or communism.

At the end of the nineties the insular, economically desperate Chinese reached out to the West. By 2001 China joined the World Trade Organization. The ruling party of China had no desire to end up like the Soviets. It chose the Hegelian synthesis and it has worked well, making cheap goods for American and European consumers, using industrial factories run like slave labor camps, massive currency manipulation, and theft of intellectual property. The fat corrupted West turned out to be easy pickings as China moved to replace America as the world's supreme superpower.

But internal contradictions in China, combined with the looming demographic disaster, portend an ominous future not only for them, but those nations that are heavily invested there.

But that doesn't dissuade the left from anointing China as the new model. No one expressed the need to get rid of democracy more enthusiastically than United Nations Climate Chief, Christiana Figueres, who stated emphatically in January of 2014, and with a sense of dizzying tyrannical absolutism, that democracy was a poor political system for fighting global warming. China, and its one party fascistic paradise, she insisted, is the best model. China, the world's greatest polluter, adamantly agreed.

Without its own deep entrepreneurial culture, China has no choice but to steal technology by cracking into every computer and business in America. It's about growing the power necessary for its great ambition to replace America as the world's superpower, a mission Figueres strongly agrees with.

FOR THE LEFTIST COGNOSCENTI of Europe and America, all roads lead back to Hegel's *'Dialectics of History'* and Marx's *'Dialectical Materialism'*, the architecture of the greatest mass State murders in modern history, errors to be corrected by this new bright and shiny hope-and-change welfare state synthesis.

For many Americans, following Europe down the rabbit hole is suicide.

America was once upon a time dominated by tinkerers, explorers and entrepreneurs. They are being replaced by the new age of *thinkers* who want to radically change this nation and the world at large into a new, multicultural socially engineered paradise.

This miracle transformation requires building a happy working class of wealth producing techies supporting massive government and a joyful class of dependent artists, gangbangers and California surfers who only need a monthly stipend to pursue their ecstatic existence without having to be 'job locked'.

And yes, robots are coming to do all the small jobs, so get ready for 'free' freedom, where nothing is required of a person other than supporting the soft bosom of the Superstate as it supports you.

In the pursuit of greater good of this new paradise all power must be in the hands of a permanent class of overseers. This secular priesthood is to make sure that climate change, social justice, and world peace arrive soon. For that to happen, the opposition that is stalling the arrival of nirvana, those old fashion traditionalists, must be silenced.

Much of the hostile resentment and envy that the elite gold-star class has against those who actually create the technological world will finally end when these leftist *wunderkinds* are celebrated and properly worshipped as they pursue their manifest destiny to rebuild society on the rubble of this once great nation.

It is incomprehensible to the gold-star Hope and Change all-knowing new progressive elite that anyone could be so pathetically stupid as to resist the coming of a vast tribal community that seeks social justice, equality, diversity, multicultural love and peace and the end to the hated 'white privilege.'

Yes, these evil 'white privileged' people may have invented pretty much every technology the modern world uses, but it was done on the graves of Native Americans, and on the backs of African/Americans and the poor. They must be yanked down off their proverbial high horse.

A WEAKENED AND STRESSED AMERICA finds itself having an ideological nervous breakdown as it lurches about like a wounded animal, and like all wounded animals invites predation.

The philosophical battle taking place is between a modern version of the old German and French 'command and control' Statism, and the free market, small government vision that reached fruition in this leftist hated land.

Individualism versus collectivism has always been the center of that ideological conflict in the West. Who wins determines the sovereignty of the people, or the dominance of the state.

A constitutional republic that elevated the

individual over the state, while creating the biggest and most successful commercial society in history, has always been the enemy of the world's elitists.

The refusal to accept this great hybrid of capitalism and socialism and the defeat of the 'idea' that built America is the essence of the struggle.

If government, as progressives insist, is responsible for all of creation then why didn't socialist and communist governments become the wealthiest, most productive in history, rather than history's greatest failures and murderous disasters?

If government built everything, how did the first folks here without any government in Washington survive without road builders like Harry Reid and Nancy Pelosi?

Certainly, government uses the wealth extracted from the capitalist economy to land on the moon, build great highway systems, and fight wars. But that wealth must be created before it can be extracted for other purposes.

From the wilderness to the present, the real builders are creative inventors, explorers and entrepreneurs for whom government could extract and use wealth and inventions and organize great expeditions. Putting them under the control of the state will end their ability to create and produce.

The great contradiction of the progressive left lies in their ambition to create a communal collective that will cut off the hand that feeds them, which is the freedom of entrepreneurial capitalism. The mountain of regulations they impose expands government and its appetite shrinks the means by which government is fed. We once went to the moon, now we hitch rides on Russian rockets.

Collectivist nations have never been successful in their own right. They succeed to a degree by copying the ideas and inventions of free market economies, while running up massive debt and building empires of corruption. America is the victim of the greatest international thieves in history, and much of it is the fault of this nation's incredibly stupid leaders and their crony capitalist handlers.

Conservative Dinesh D'Souza, widely reviled by the left, said in his movie and the book *'Obama's America'*, "This country, once an experiment unique in the world, is now the last best hope of the World."

If there is any chance of defeating the progressive ideology, it will not come from the halls of power among Washington Republicans, nor from the Tea Party and its allies, but ultimately from an awakening in the American universities and coffee shops and across social media among millennials, the largest generation in our history.

This nation emerged from the Renaissance and Reformation, the Hanseatic League and the rise of English individualism, leading to the greatest economic and political system the world has ever known. A revolution much of the world has yet to experience.

This great battle will be won or lost in the schools and universities where the entrenched leftist catechism has reigned for decades. If not seriously challenged, America will be defeated and its great 'idea' lost.

As Lincoln made clear, what is taught in the schools becomes what is later practiced in government. We are experiencing exactly that. Who wins the millennials wins the war and that war is raging in the schools.

EIGHT

THE CATECHISM
OF STATE SUPREMACY

But every politically controlled educational system will inculcate the doctrine of state supremacy sooner or later, whether as the divine right of kings, or the 'will of the people' in 'democracy'. Once that doctrine has been accepted, it becomes an almost superhuman task to break the stranglehold of the political power over the life of the citizen.

–Isabel Paterson, *The God of the Machine*

THE PROGRESSIVES UNDERSTOOD the critical need to put a stranglehold on the educational system. They had a vision of a radical spin on the motto of the Great Seal of the United States—*NOVUS ORDO SECLORUM*—a new order of the ages. That could only come from getting control of the minds of the young.

This new order is being promoted by the 60s neo-

Marxists radicals who are now the dominant force in the education system. They represent the statist takeover of what was once a local system and their focus isn't on education so much as indoctrination.

In 1980, Jimmy Carter created the Department of Education. Departmentalizing education seems contrary to our history and reason, but is necessary for ultimate control in the pursuit of liberal manifest destiny.

The funding has gone up ever since, and the progress of students has gone in the opposite direction. Bureaucracy doing what it does best.

The failing students isn't a problem as long as their radicalization continues. Establishing progressive control over society and how society thinks, not actual education, is the real goal and that has been very successful.

WHO DEFINES RULES and American history is now written by those who define our history as steeped in oppression, theft, slavery and genocide. This new politically correct catechism has replaced old-fashion patriotism, mocked as ridiculous, racist and structurally hostile to multicultural diversity.

America built a Constitution and Bill of Rights around the common person, not the elite, the private world, not the public world and local education was a big part.

The defeat of America, Lincoln suggested, in agreement with the Founders, will come from within, not by some foreign power. And 'within' nothing is more critical than the schools and the press. But both have abjectly surrendered to the PC culture.

Noam Chromsky, himself no fan of America, or its capitalistic economic system, said it as well as anyone: "The smart way to keep people passive and obedient is to strictly limit the acceptable opinion, but allow very lively debate within that spectrum."

Political correctness is about creating the boundaries of discussion and thought. It's soft fascism, a shadow of what will follow if progressive power becomes fully consolidated.

All over American campuses we see phony outrage over such subsequent issues as not serving authentic cultural foods, or offensive Halloween costumes. There is growing hostility to the first amendment, ending free speech, creating 'safe zones', i.e., leftist zones where the spineless in this generation can avoid offensiveness while sitting around holding hands and loving one another like a bunch of clueless kindergarteners. Their leaders are administrators and professors who were reared in the fermented juices of the Maoist 60s.

An awakening of the stronger students is slowly beginning to emerge as a counterforce, but not yet a serious challenge.

The predators of the world look upon American

campuses and smile with delight. It's going to be easier pickings in the near future than they could ever have imagined.

INSTALLING AN INTERNAL SENSOR in young minds to achieve political correctness from grade school through the universities is the ultimate goal of progressive education.

As the Catholics used to say—give us the first seven years and we have them for life. All religions operate on the principle of installing correct values, but in a free society like America religions don't and can't suppress freedom of action, expression or thought.

Secular progressive ideology, on the other hand, seeks to limit those freedoms. In concert with fascism, socialism and radical Islam the ultimate goal is suppression on all those fronts.

The early religiosity of Americans has always accepted the concept of freedom of thought and expression as a political right and a core value. That is no longer true. Either you believe in the revealed truths and ambitions of the left or you're condemned, shunned, despised.

The suppression begins slow and soft, but grows. In the PC dominated university, culture thought and open discussions are only allowed within certain accepted parameters. Everything outside these accepted parameters is considered a form of 'hate' speech.

A classic example happened at UC Santa Cruz, Stevens College. Students attending a fun 'inter-galactic' conference about inter-galactic aliens happened to have insensitively ordered Mexican food, a favorite while discussing cosmic aliens. This triggered a protest at the insensitivity. How dare one talk about any kind of aliens, 'inter-galactic' or otherwise, and yet not sense the micro-aggression involved?

There could be no greater crime than the breakdown of the PC sensitivity sensor. So the conference was cancelled, thus displaying the intellectually crippling power of ideological tyranny.

Political correctness is the top concern on many campuses. Once newer programs like Common Core take full effect in the lower grades, thus further nationalizing education and removing local controls, the victory and dominance of progressive political agenda will follow.

Local expressions of old fashion patriotism, religious values and personal virtues, common in our past, will effectively be condemned as an evil shield for 'white privilege'.

THE WAR AGAINST CHARTER SCHOOLS by Democratic mayors in big cities with large black populations, such as the socialist Bill de Blasio in NYC, display a lack of interest in the actual academic performance of inner city kids. What they seek, behind all the love and tolerance for diversity is to maintain political control of a major voting bloc.

Any movement toward individualized instruction has to be stopped. A tribe can't exist with freedom of thought or action that are not approved by the leaders.

The near total abandonment of the battle on campus by conservatives and traditionalists over the past thirty years left the field wide open for the dominance of progressive ideology. No longer is freedom of thought and expression allowed to wander very far off the PC educational plantation.

As the highly respected liberal constitutional scholar Johnathan Turley said, "College campuses have recently seemed more like centers of political re-education than real learning. . ."

When universities replace free speech with correct speech, progressive campuses begin to resemble those in China. They stole our technology, we're stealing their oppression.

On many progressive American campuses conservative speakers are routinely disinvited from speaking as they will cause anxiety among some of the very sensitive who can't tolerate 'micro-aggressions'.

Books, many of them classics, containing *'micro-aggressions'* now need *'trigger warnings'* about what might promote discomfort for students who will read them.

Babysitting the little munchkin boys and girls—if they can thus be sexually divided—is the main job of administrators today. Our campuses don't yet have loudspeakers in the morning, afternoon, and evening booming socialist thought, as villages in China do, but that may come in the not too distant future.

The transformative ambition of the collective is to replace selfish individualism, i.e., human nature, with altruistic selflessness and personal ambition with collective ambition as determined by the high priests of the social justice Superstate.

THE REPUBLIC'S FOUNDERS chose to construct a political, social and economic architecture that would channel human nature and competitive energy in the most positive, creative way, through universal law under a constitution and Bill of Rights that allowed freedom while protecting against predation.

By restricting the power of the state, the Founding Fathers unleashed the power of a sovereign people. It proved to be unequaled. Almost every major advance in technology used around the world came from the streets, garages and homes of Americans.

William Bradford's early mistake, one he was forced to correct to save the colony, has now been brought back under the guise of the new Democratic

Socialism, an oxymoron if there ever was one.

The purpose of government in America wasn't to *purify* society, it was to engineer a political architecture that would *protect* society both from itself, and from foreign enemies.

Education was local and not a venture for re-educating the human race to follow true believers down the yellow brick road for a political picnic on the sands of the sea of love only to get wiped out by a blood-dimmed tide.

Historically, the catechism in most American schools was built on the 'idea' of a republic whose architecture was to prevent absolutism. Students were taught not so much what to think, but how to think, not what to read, but how to read. And they were to prepare all through their education for a future career in the marketplace. And beneath it all had to be some kind of moral base of values and virtues and personal responsibility, or else the republic couldn't long survive.

As *'The True Believer'* author Eric Hoffer put it, "We have rudiments of reverence for the human body, but we consider as nothing the rape of the human mind."

Progressive control of how the nation thinks, how it defines words and thoughts, is the key to establishing the tyranny of social justice. Co-opting definitions, changing the meaning of words and events of history to fit their ideological narrative.

Liberal now means welfare state collectivism. Food stamps are supplemental nutrition assistance. Freedom is not being 'job locked'.

It's all part of the new progressive catechism for America whose endgame is absolute power in the hands of the state. As Lord Acton popularly suggested, "All power corrupts, but absolute power corrupts absolutely."

There is a nearly irresistible attraction to power by those who believe in their moral mission to fix the world. They are the new priesthood of the politically correct secular religion that wants to impose their radical vision for the greater good.

The greatest danger to any society originates with the ambition of delusional leaders on a quixotic mission that engages deceived masses, and demands a tyranny in the pursuit of the greater good administered by a righteous ruling elite of arrogant moral busybodies.

NINE

A TYRANNY OF
MORAL BUSYBODIES

...a tyranny exercised for the good of its victims may be the most oppressive. It may be better to live under the robber barons than under omnipotent moral busybodies.

–C.S. Lewis

CONSERVATIVE ICON RONALD REAGAN delivered what he said were the nine scariest words, "I'm from the government and I'm here to help."

Are those words just humorous, not scary in this moment in American history? Are Americans so disconnected from the values of the past that they are now willing subjects to the government's relentless helping hand?

Careful what you wish for, the critics of the social justice Superstate advise. Once these moralistic warriors enter your life in order to better it, they own your life, and getting it back will be no easy task. Even worse, you set up future generations to be born into a form of permanent indentured servitude to the State.

OBAMA'S HARDCORE ACOLYTES who occupy the seat of the greatest power on earth came to Washington possessed by a sense of their manifest destiny to impose their vision on society, whether society liked it or not. These selfless crusaders insisted on the necessary power, taken one way or another, to bring forth the new world of their dreams, their subjective 'state of mind' objectified by possession of moral authority and absolute power.

The constitutional opposition's view is that the great miseries of modern times aren't the result of roadside villains, corporate swindlers, oil barons, or Dick Cheney. They are the result of delusional visions that require massive power to attempt to bring about their dreams.

The neo-Marxists of our time insist those bad old mass-murder days are so last century. In this new Marx-lite era there would be no more Gulags, gas chambers, or labor camps. Given complete control of the major education institutions and the cooperation of the submissive media, such harsh tactics wouldn't be necessary. So much has been learned from those dark days that everyone will see, understand, and cooperate   in   the   pursuit   of   social   justice, environmentalism and global, antiwar tranquility.

Those angry terrorists in the Middle East are simply the product of climate change, joblessness, and the terrible oil greed that stole their beautiful Bedouin heritage. Their anger will subside and they'll eventually make peace once they see America's new rulers and good intentions. Their violence and genocide has nothing to do with Islam and everything to do with America and its global hegemony.

Those Americans who object to that analysis have to be dealt with. It might be necessary to get a little rough with the rise of rightwing resistance, the real enemy. These recalcitrant rebels have to either be brought back into line or crushed by endless ridicule and attacked by agencies like the IRS, Homeland Security, the NSA and Harry Reid.

HUMAN NATURE'S CHALLENGE demands intelligent reaction to the playing field given, with the values taught, or learned by hard experience. Survival's challenges and responses create victory or defeat, prosperity or poverty.

From mankind's reptilian base to the highest levels of its creative genius we are always challenged. The greatest miseries have come from ideological and religious fanaticism, followed by raging diseases and predatory wars.

History's sad lament is that those posing as man's

altruistic liberators become man's biggest jailers. German poet Fredrich Holderlin, once a roommate of Hegel's, succinctly and brilliantly put it, "What has always made the State a hell on earth has been precisely that man has tried to make it his heaven."

The radical left, obsessed with their vision and their elite position in society, mocked Henry David Thoreau's insistence that the government that governs least governs best. The progressives truly believed that, given enough power, they could create their vision of heaven on earth. The restrictions of small government in a republic contradict everything they stand for.

Democracy, without the restraints of a republic to channel and restrict the energy of power, easily becomes mobocracy. Pure democracy is a dangerous myth and no one showed it better than the mass murderers of the last century.

F.A. Hayek observed that Hitler didn't have to destroy democracy, as it had already decayed and people wanted a powerful vision of a new world with leaders to get them there. Over and over again that has been the story of the rise of popular tyrants preaching salvation through revolution.

People who feel the nation heading in the wrong direction, crushing their ambition want change and set about creating organizations from the grassroots to bring it about.

But there are others who feel weak and

threatened but want strength, not from themselves and their ability to organize, but from some radical new collective movement promising some airy socialist vision. They are taught that the problem is the constitutional republic itself. They are the generation feared by the Founders, one that has been educated with progressive thinking and are seeking revolutionary transition in themselves and the world.

The fanatic mindset of the most willing to become soldiers in a new political army, one seeking tyrannical powers in the name of social revolution, is brilliantly described in Eric Hoffer's quintessential '*The True Believer*':

"There is apparently some connection between dissatisfaction with oneself and a proneness to credulity. The urge to escape our real self is also an urge to escape the rational and the obvious. The refusal to see ourselves as we are develops a distaste for facts and cold logic. There is no hope for the frustrated in the actual and the possible. Salvation can come to them only from the miraculous, which seeps through a crack in the iron wall of inexorable reality. They ask to be deceived. What Stresemann said of the Germans is true of the frustrated in general: '*They pray not only for their daily bread, but also for their daily illusion.*' The rule seems to be that those who find no difficulty in deceiving themselves are easily deceived by others. They are easily persuaded and led."

This mindset is evident in the rise of the radical

progressive movement in America where the most ardent followers care nothing about facts or reality, but everything about myths and falsely based emotions that appear to satisfy some underlying hunger for submission to feel-good illusions and a new identity.

There are always charismatic tyrants willing to satisfy that hunger for revolutionary transformation within one's self and provide a movement within which one can merge and trade a sense of individual weakness for collective strength.

Given the underlying intensity of the struggle we face over who should run our world, from education to politics and economics, it is a battle over the very 'idea' at the center of America's core values, the very soul of the republic.

POWER CLOAKED IN SELFLESSNESS is the ultimate aphrodisiac. It demands worshipful peasants marching together down the road to a delusional paradise. It is nothing short of a complete religification of politics.

Isabel Paterson reflected, "The lust for power is most easily disguised under humanitarian or philanthropic motives."

In the pursuit of a tribal communal tyranny, many will forsake everything that made them a free people in the hopes of some vision with no basis in reality.

America writhes in the grip of the greatest power grab by its central government over the destiny of the citizenry in our history and, as usual, it is cloaked in altruism.

Altruism in politics leads to selfless submission to tyranny. The author of 'Atlas Shrugged' conservative/libertarian Ayn Rand, much reviled by the radical left, stated, "If any civilization is to survive, it is the morality of altruism that men have to reject."

Those who exercise power on moral grounds always end up demanding submission to the needs of authority. It is totally antithetical to the political ideology that created the greatest social and economic power the world has ever known.

In the mindset of the progressives, it was their time, one of revolutionary transformation. In every speech, in every sentiment, they mocked Edmond Burke's warning, "the greater the power the more dangerous the abuse."

It didn't apply to them. They were special because they were pure, and their purity was based on the belief that the evils of the world could be eradicated by social programs put forth by the selfless, progressive gold-star elite in power. When challenged in any serious way their inner ruthlessness pushed them in Alinsky attack mode.

Eric Hoffer adds, "The hatred and cruelty which have their source in selfishness are ineffectual things compared with the venom and ruthlessness born of selflessness."

EXTREME POWER IS THE CHILD OF CRISES that demand power to solve major problems. But however deep the sword of power cuts into modern society it must be wrapped in the moral cloth of the greater good.

Crisis is the constant means for power's justification. Crisis is the cocaine of power. Nothing sustains power like a crisis that is perpetual, like climate change. But there are times when the experts of crisis might have to deal with one of their own making.

As Rahm Emanuel advised during his time in Washington, never let a crisis go to waste. After his return from the White House to the Chicago's mayoral office he faced an election and suppressed a video of a police officer shooting a black man sixteen times. It got him elected. A year after his election when the video finally surfaced this master of the crisis was forced to face one of his own making.

WHAT REPLACES TRUTH in the new progressive order is whatever fictional narrative is necessary in the pursuit and preservation of power.

Plato, no fan of individualism or freedom, suggested, as Karl Popper pointed out: ". . . of the group, or of the tribe; it is not individual selfishness, but it is collective selfishness." That is a near perfect description of the moral basis of all totalitarian regimes. The group is everything, the individual, nothing.

The progressives of our time rose from neo-Marxists, anti-war 60s. They were the Boomers of that era who rebelled against LBJ's war and draft and expounded the communism of Mao Tse-tung, one of history's greatest mass murderers. Add Karl Marx's, *'The Communist Manifesto'* and *'Das Kapital,'* and you have much of the underlying philosophical base for horrors that the world still isn't past.

When Democratic Socialist Bernie Sanders and his bride honeymooned in the bloody Soviet Union he didn't take a free room in the Gulag Archipelago. Way too many ghosts running about there.

The descendants of the radical 60's boomers, took over the White House with a passionate mission nothing short of a historic transformation of America into the new Hegelian compromise: socialists in control of the capitalist machine's purposes.

No grassroots movement of lesser beings was going to stop the radicals once in power. They would use whatever means at their disposal to destroy the opposition in the name of social justice.

The rapture of power legitimizes deception in the pursuit of greater truths. No one is better at lies, big lies and noble lies than the heirs of Saul Alinsky and his *'Rules for Radicals'*, the definitive bible of the Obama regime and Hilary Clinton as she fights off the many rightwing conspiracies that, in her mind, are constantly dropping out of the dark skies to attack her beautiful flower garden of lies.

If the millennials awaken from their slumber they will face a gigantic mess built on delusions and noble lies. And they will have to begin asking serious questions.

TEN

LIES, BIG LIES & NOBLE LIES

*In a time of universal deceit—telling the truth
is a revolutionary act.*

–George Orwell

THE PROGRESSIVE AGENDA DEMANDS the
constant use of narrative lies. They are not only
morally justified, lies are absolutely demanded in the
pursuit of the noble outcome. The despised enemy
must be defeated at all costs, that enemy being
conservative/libertarian, constitutional, fly-over
America and its evil, regressive values.

While truth is the first casualty of war, in
contemporary progressive politics, it's war all the time
and truth is never in play.

The ascent of the politically correct to victory is
the only relevancy, as that 'truther' Harry Reid made
crystal clear when confronted about his senate lie

concerning Romney's taxes during that republican's presidential bid against Obama. It was all about winning, this custodian of virtue stated emphatically, not about truth.

Lies are instruments to gain victory over those who are opposed to the ultimate truths that only real insiders possess.

PROGRESSIVE MORAL SUPERIORITY requires no rationale beyond itself for demanding the power necessary to carry out the greater good. In the far left's ideological subjectivism reality is creatively manufactured, altered or distorted, as needed in the drive to create the *greater truth*, which will be unveiled once reviled domestic enemies like the Tea Party, Fox News, talk radio, the Koch Brothers, and conservative voices in general, are muted.

When a government goes to war against large segments of its population in an effort to create a new social framework, the first order of business is to defeat those who resist this new centralized 'command and control' nirvana run by gold-star masterminds, not just defeat them, but obliterate their causes, their presence, their voice.

Fortunately for the radical left, the right is so busy fighting among themselves they may well self-destruct on their own.

BIG AND NOBLE LIES ARE TOOLS necessary for building the revolutionary new society. When a big lie is repeated over and over, ad infinitum, and not challenged by the media, those lies begin to be accepted as facts. As Heir Hitler advised, "The great masses will more easily fall victim to a big lie than a small one."

In America, the average citizen can be manipulated, attacked and relentlessly shamed for past crimes, leading to demoralization and submission—up to a point. But when that tipping point is reached, America's DNA awakens. Then serious blowback becomes inevitable.

For the progressive politico it doesn't matter that the crimes in question, such as the Ferguson lie, have no basis in fact. What matters is the ability to turn every narrative, true or false, into one which will work to trash, weaken and shame to death the opposition.

–White privilege and structural racism
–The Benghazi video
–Keep your doctor and health plan
–Al Qaeda on the run, ISIS contained
–Iraq and Yemen are great victories
–The VA takes care of veterans
–Lois Lerner's emails just vanished
–Hillary's emails innocently deleted
–Terrorists aren't Islamic

Lies well crafted, half-truths well-rehearsed, cover-ups and diversions constantly repeated by the talking heads and their support teams, are the progressive's life blood. And the greatest of lies is the Noble Lie from which the ultimate truth will emerge.

NOBLE LIES ARE THE CARPET BOMBS of political war. As George Orwell stated, "Political language is designed to make lies sound truthful and murder respectable, and to give an appearance of solidity to pure wind."

Lying on behalf of the noble goal has been used down through the ages to support tyranny. Social justice, progressives insist, will be visible only when the evil mists of 'white' privilege and rightwing Christian fanaticism withdraw. Then, and only then, will their shining Camelot be fully realized and the hidden 'real' truth revealed.

Citizens simply must have faith in the grand narrative and accept what they are told, and that means accept the lies in the hope the change that the progressives promise isn't some pathetic, university created mirage, but in fact the 'real' truth behind the necessary lies.

OBAMACARE IS A CLASSIC EXAMPLE of a

noble lie that came down upon society out of the night while the nation slept.

Jonathan Gruber, one of the chief authors, defended the deception and night rollout as necessary because the average America was *just too stupid* to understand that level of sophistication. Only he and his elite brethren had the necessary brain power.

Besides, it's a major piece of the Obama's shining legacy, and being the first 'black' president no one can get in the way of that legacy, otherwise they are showing their racism.

How this healthcare system would be administered, paid for or even constitutional, wasn't relevant. What mattered, besides Obama's obsession with his personal legacy, was the advance of government dominance over a sixth of the economy, another step in the direction of the ultimate government control of your life and society.

Leftists ignored Thomas Jefferson's warning about great innovations being forced on slender majorities, which is why Obamacare had to be done in the middle of the night. In the morning light, constitutionalists would see the monster as the greatest single unconstitutional imposition on the nation in America's history. And they would get angry.

In a supreme insult to that document, Supreme Court justice John Roberts engineered a fraudulent decision to make Obamacare a tax and handed it over to that most corrupt of agencies, the IRS. He explained in a pathetically weak argument that he didn't want the people upset with the court, as if that was somehow constitutionally relevant.

A voice came out of the darkness of the House that assured the nation. "We have to pass the bill so that you can find out what is in it," blithely babbled the bubbly democratic house whip, Nancy Pelosi, insulting democracy and sanity. Those words came out of her mouth like the flickering silver tongue of a venomous snake striking at the heart of America.

And it was just the beginning. Right from the start, secret plans were already in the works to open the borders and bring in millions who would be rewarded with healthcare, schooling, driver's licenses, and all the goodies of regular citizens.

The Obama progressives had no qualms about imposing their will on society without the usual, boring constitutional protections. The great transformative mission was everything. They had little serious establishment Republican opposition.

AMERICA'S RADICALIZED MEDIA turned reporting into a propaganda wing of the Obama administration. They supported the lies while ignoring anything that might be negative. In one of the most egregious dereliction of duty, they abandoned any attempt to be objective, thus driving a knife into the heart of a republic that demands independence of the media in order to survive.

This refusal to pursue objectivity and truth by the media reached levels of criminal negligence and moral treason unprecedented in our history.

The Paris attacks that occurred late in Obama's second term created some anxiety among a few in the media. Even more when they bore witness to their president showing far greater interest in climate change and golf, then heads falling or genocide against Christians.

The shocking mass murder by a radical Islamic couple in San Bernardino, California, followed by Obama's bizarre Sunday night ramble, created a bit more angst in the liberal media, but they were trapped. They couldn't abandon their president as they had invested everything in him and his vision and their abject submission. They were solidly hooked. Even his shocking justification for a lack of reaction to the attacks in Brussels by continuing to watch a baseball game with communist dictator, Raul Castro in Cuba, then the next day, demonstrating his tango inabilities in Argentina, garnered momentary press negativity, that soon vanished, except on FOX news.

They had bought early and deeply into the sophomoric delusions of the administration and couldn't turn against it as that would be an admission of utter abject failure, not only of judgment, but of their credentials as journalists.

But disturbing news concerning Hillary Clinton's emails, her foundation, and the rise of serious, socialist opposition among the young college students tightened the trap the progressive media was caught in, and it just got tighter by the day, exits closing fast.

PROGRESSIVE MANIFEST DESTINY demands a foreign policy that puts blame for all miseries in the world on America's doorstep. Those who are foolish enough to point to factual realities are subject to every kind of vicious attack by the subjectivist revolutionaries.

As Socrates, quoting from Plato's Republic put it, "The noble lie is: *a contrivance for one of those falsehoods that come into being in case of need . . . some noble one.*"

–The soldiers/contractors who tried to describe what happened in the *13 Hours,* attacked

–The soldiers in Afghanistan who tried to tell what they knew about Bergdahl's desertion, attacked

–The Fort Hood shooter workplace violence

–The man who killed Bin Laden under investigative intimidation for appearing on Fox

And, in a freakish ultimate alternate universe of re-definitions, the Taliban, those murderers of school children, agents of endless violence against women, long-time supporters of the likes of al Qaeda, are not really terrorists, according to Principal Deputy Press Secretary Eric Schultz. He explained that we don't negotiate with terrorists. These nice folks were just a bunch of misguided *armed insurgents,* with whom we are allowed to negotiate, justifying the exchange of five high-grade Gitmo terrorists for deserter Sgt. Bergdahl.

Later, our sailors on their knees, guns at their heads as the Iranians filmed the humiliation and showed it around the world, our ever apologetic Secretary of State John Kerry gushed with praise and happy thankfulness to the Iranians who were gracious enough to return the illegally captured sailors. This came a week before the release of sanctions and the 150 billion dollars to our new Iranian buddies.

Yes, Kerry agreed, some of those billions would go to terrorism, but that's the way of things when you're trying to build a better world. You have to compromise, bow, drop to your knees and hope for the best.

And to further that affection, Obama visited a radical mosque in Maryland known for its ties to the Islamic Brotherhood just days after the 2016 Iowa primary, to let them know we cannot allow anti-Islamic hate speech. He got big applause.

LIE, ATTACK, AND DEFLECT in order to define all opposition as part of some vast rightwing conspiracy. To the true Hegelian subjectivist, reality is what you will it to be. Scientists, inventors, entrepreneurs can't avoid reality. On the other hand, political scientists, sociologists, politicians and the media can, and do so, on a regular basis. No one has told more lies in politics than Hillary Clinton:

–Ducking bullets in Bosnia
–Bengazhi caused by a video
–She and Bill left the White House dead broke
–No emails marked 'top secret'
–Grandparents are all immigrants

And on and on go the lies into the dimming vapors of a condition that, after a half century of practice, with Alinsky cheering her on from the grave, she now can't see truth if it is staring her in the face. That's a near pathological condition.

A SERIOUS POLITICAL CRISIS emerged with the loss of the House and the Senate to Republicans in Obama's second term. The president had to make a major move away from democracy to save his legacy. Nothing can stand in the way of manifest destiny.

He needed to move on to the next phase of power and become what he always dreamed of, becoming an Imperial President.

As political *wunderkinder* actress Gwyneth Paltrow

gushed at a Hollywood party, the president should take *all the power* he needs to carry out his mission. What dictator wouldn't love that submissive affection from such a beautiful admirer?

Obama assured his gushing fan and the country, that he would rule imperially by 'executive orders,' pen-and-phone in hand, in order to chisel his legacy in stone regardless of the cost to the constitution and a nation he had no great love for to start with. He was very much in sync with Gwyneth and Hollywood.

ELEVEN

THE IMPERIAL PRESIDENT

When people fear the government, there is tyranny.
When the government fears the people, there is liberty.

–Thomas Jefferson

OBAMA RULED WITH HIS 'PEN-AND-PHONE' like some banana republic dictator, as he'd promised Gwyneth. He issued one executive order after another in defiance of constitutional restraint, and with virtually no serious opposition from the establishment Republicans who had adjusted quite well to massive government expansion.

When the political laws of the land no longer emerge from the House and Senate, are no longer in contact or concert with the people, but are functions of bureaucracies and the phone-and-pen imperial presidency, it's a new era and a lawless one for the average person. It feels much more like the beginning of a dictatorship where agencies control of one's social, economic and political existence.

Beyond the big legacy issues like healthcare, open borders, and sanctuary cities, closing Gitmo, the disastrous, premature pullout of troops from the Middle East wars, came an avalanche of strangling regulations. They dropped out of the stellar heights of the centralized command-and-control government through bloated agencies run by career bureaucrats.

The more Obama imposed without serious blowback, the more he and his loyal inner circle of sycophants realized just how easy it was to dictate to the once greatest and freest nation on earth.

It was as if an American generation had emerged that had no fundamental identity and was begging to be led by a new gospel and new preacher.

After the catastrophe of the Vietnam War, 9/11, the mess of the Iraq War, and the housing collapse that took the nation into a serious recession, Americans fell for Hope and Change.

In Las Vegas in a speech in 2011, Obama warned the nation that he would canvass agencies for actions similar to what Bill Clinton did, only in a much bigger way. Obama sought to create regulations for everything from retirement accounts to EPA climate actions, immigration, and dozens and dozens of other rules and regulations that gave the bureaucracies a more powerful grip on the nation.

He was straightforward. He had power and

intended to use it to the max in pursuit of his ideological visions. No hubris climbs the heights of power and pretention like the pursuit of the greater good in the hands of a delusional leader. Especially when a nation feels confused and lost.

Protected by race and a fawning media, Obama didn't have to reach across isles to work with anyone. He had the American stage all to himself. He wanted big government and now was a time like no other to make it happen. Few politicians in our history have had an open stage with no serious opposition.

Bill Clinton, under the powerful influence of Newt Gingrich's 'Contract with America', announced a decade earlier, in between trysts, that the era of big government was over.

Obama brought big government back with a vengeance. He spent more money in large programs than any leader in history, including all the previous presidents combined—adding a massive 10 trillion dollars to the already bloated debt left by Bush. He became King Obama.

The arms of the progressive Leviathan now reached hungrily into all corners of the republic in order to feed its insatiable appetite, and when called on, destroy internal enemies.

The president's dedicated disciples had no qualms about using every method and means to frighten and crush opposition. From the IRS assault on the Tea Party to the outrageous midnight raids in Wisconsin by police and investigators smashing down doors and frightening the inhabitants of conservative homes, and then denying the people in those homes the right to speak to anyone about their ordeal.

This outrageous, fascistic action revealed in David French's article in the National Review titled 'Wisconsin's shame', showed naked tyranny in action. A new dark era rising.

UNRESTRICTED IMMIGRATION was the progressive's fast track to expanding the future progressive political base. With thousands of unassimilable refugees from the collapse of Obama's policies in the Middle East, we'll have a crisis similar to that in Europe.

America is changing and fast. It will not be the republic of the Founding Fathers unless something radical happens to reverse course. The great 'idea' of the republic is on life support.

In the former democratic governor of Colorado, Richard D. Lamm's satirical essay, *'I have a secret plan to destroy America'*, one of his six methods involves making our, "fastest-growing demographic group the least educated—I would have this second underclass have a 50 percent dropout rate from school."

Other keys to destroying America in his list are to celebrate diversity over unity, multiculturalism over Western culture, and ethnic identity over American identity. They are all in play in this era of politically correct submission.

SEE SOMETHING, SAY SOMETHING was undercut by political correctness and the end result was mass murder. A neighbor of the jihadists killers who slaughtered those at the Christmas party in San Bernardino admitted she'd witnessed unusual activity for weeks leading up to the mass murder, but didn't report it for fear of being labeled anti-Islamic. Her fears may have been justified when police officers in Irving, Texas arrested 14 year old, Ahmed Mohamed, a Muslim teen who brought a bomb-looking device to school. He was given an official apology by Obama at the White House, and his family launched a $15 million dollar anti-Islamic lawsuits against the city and the school. Subsequently, Ahmed has accepted a scholarship in Qatar.

And a day after the mass shootings in San Bernardino, Loretta Lynch assured Muslims that anti-Islamic hate speech would not be tolerated and she was willing to use her prosecutorial powers, the constitution notwithstanding. Obama had indeed surrounded his administration with dedicated disciples willing to do whatever he thought necessary.

DISTURBED HEARTLAND RESIDENTS couldn't

grasp the impossible but looming notion that their president had a much more affectionate attitude toward Islam than his own country.

The idea that America built its first navy to fight Islamic radicals is not part of American education, but is part of our history, as Brian Kilmead's book, 'Thomas Jefferson and the Tripoli Pirates' reminds us. Our first navy was built by Jefferson to counter the radical Islamists in Tripoli who were capturing our trading ships and imprisoning and holding for ransom hundreds of Americans.

Jefferson went to war on sea and land, from Benghazi to Tripoli, won the campaign and came home. No nation building, just victory.

That was then. We are now in a radically different era. Obama submitted when Iran demanded a lifting of sanctions and the right to eventually build nuclear weapons. The president agreed on the principle that peace comes when you give your potential enemies what they want in return for peace. Hitler was handed the Sudetenland to calm him down. That didn't work out as Chamberlain had hoped.

Meanwhile, that great navy started by Jefferson has been torn down to a pitiful level by Obama. Some of our troops have to hitch rides from other countries to get from point A to point B. Weakening our military has been one of Obama's objectives and major successes.

TECHNOLOGY AND SOCIAL MEDIA can be great tools for liberty, or for expanding tyranny. We accept temporary restrictions of liberty in the name of protection from enemies, but resist the government's intrusion as a permanent burden. Or once did.

Obama's rule became more about the redistribution of wealth than protecting the means by which it is created, more about special interest law than universal law, and more about diminishing America's role in the world than maintaining its status as the most powerful among nations. He's winning on all fronts.

Given human nature and its problematic history, if there is one truth the Founders agreed on in that Golden Age of political thought it was that no faction, religion, utopian movement should be allowed to reach such power that it could impose, deny, dictate or control the flow of energy in the social, economic and political ecology of the society, thereby choking off freedom and productivity for individuals in order to advance the interests of special groups and the State.

The Founders understood the successes and failures of history in ways unlike any political thinkers before them, as they had a new country to create from scratch. They made a political bet that freedom, private property, and economic solvency protected by a Constitution and Bill of Rights, would do great things. They were right.

America wasn't born in dependency or tribal submission; she was born in rebellion against both. Will those instincts reemerge, or is a form of *bureaucratic servitude* now a permanent part of life in this nation as it seems always to be across Europe and the world at large?

IT'S DECISION TIME IN AMERICA and the window of opportunity to reverse course will not be open long. As Teirsais in 'Antigone' lamented: "But now you are balanced on a razor's edge."

A society under the dominating aegis of talkers and thinkers, not entrepreneurs and tinkerers, under the vast, amorphous ambitions of the State, and not the widespread ambitions and desires of those on commercial Main Street, attract hungry egos with little marketable talent, but bursting with grandiose ambition.

History has a bloody record overflowing with the horror stories of how elite intellectuals, fired up by boundless hubris, built fantastic regimes on premises utterly disconnected from reality, that pulled nations into the maw of devastation and death.

If the laws of the land are fluid, ever changing at the stroke of pen and phone, the citizen becomes by definition a victim of arbitrary power, subject to government lawlessness. Today you obeyed the law, but in the middle of the night it changed, so tomorrow you are guilty of a crime, subject to the whims of power. You are small and unimportant.

Gone is that definition of freedom, as Alexis De Tocqueville offered, "To ask anything of freedom beyond itself means one seeks to be a slave."

Freedom in the classical sense has no place in the current social justice system. It has become an irrelevant concept.

F.A. Hayek offered his opinion about the modern condition saying, "It is true that the virtues which are less esteemed and practiced now—independence, self-reliance, and the willingness to bear risks, the readiness to back one's own conviction against a majority, and the willingness to voluntary cooperation with one's neighbors—are essentially those on which the individualist society rests."

Collectivism has nothing to put in their place, and in so far as it already has destroyed, it has left a void filled by nothing but the demand for obedience and the compulsion of the individual to do what is collectively decided to be good.

When national heroes are no longer inventors, creators, entrepreneurial capitalists, but imperial politicians, then the experiment in freedom is over and John Galt, Ayn Rand's capitalist hero in '*Atlas Shrugged*', sits on death row awaiting execution.

TWELVE

KILLING JOHN GALT

*The people of the United States are more prosperous . . .
because their government embarked later than other
governments . . . upon the policy of obstructing business.*

—L. von Mises, *The Anti-capitalistic Mentality*

AMERICAN CAPITALISM CREATED a swarming ecology of inventions, experiments, ever-expanding trade like nothing the world had ever seen before. And that enormous engine of production would help build and protect the modern world and bring down her enemies.

As Isabel Paterson pointed out in her brilliant book, *'The God of the Machine'*, "Personal liberty is the pre-condition of the release of energy. Private property is the inductor which initiates the flow. Real money is the transmission line; and the payment of debts comprises half the circuit."

Capitalism grew out of the Reformation and Renaissance after a long, bitter struggle through the Dark Ages. The defeat of Usury, coupled with a sustained financial and banking rebellion in Florence in the 14th Century that then expanded through the Hanseatic League, would mature in the Protestant rebellion, Calvinism and Jewish banking, until full-blown market capitalism came to fruition in America.

Poverty, the norm for millennia, suddenly faced the most powerful economic and social revolution in history, one that opened up the entrepreneurial environment, giving rise to a commercial middle class full of tinkerers, inventors, bankers and shopkeepers. A poor immigrant could become wealthy, their children even wealthier. Nothing like America had ever happened before. Poverty was no longer the accepted norm.

When president Obama insulted this greatest entrepreneurial system on earth by proclaiming, "*You didn't build that,*" the obvious question was, who did? Why, government, of course. A sentiment echoed by the likes of that famous road builder and pseudo Indian, Elizabeth Warren.

Obama was simply echoing what he'd been taught by the radical progressive anti-capitalism of his long-time leftist friends, heirs to Saul Alinsky and the 60s would-be Maoist revolutionaries.

From Ben Franklin's kite and the horse and buggy, to trains, planes and Henry Ford's automobiles, from the telegraph to Steve Jobs, from sea-to-shining-sea and on to the moon, we're in the land of explorers, creators, and inventors who created a new kind of society based on individual freedom.

It was like telling Thomas Edison, with his 1,093 US patents—after his twenty-one thousand experiments while existing more on naps than real sleep, struggling beyond comprehension with relentless determination to a point of total obsession, until he finally succeeded in creating the light bulb that electrified the world, the movie camera, phonography, and the carbon microphone—that it was all made possible by the bureaucratic blockheads in Washington, when in fact, it the end result of the American free market.

GOVERNMENT USES THE WEALTH generated by capitalism, not bureaucrats, to accomplish major objectives.

Lincoln would ask the North to defeat the South, and they would do so because of the North's capitalist economic superiority over the plantation economy of the slave south.

FDR would ask American capitalism to ramp up production to fight and defeat Axis powers.

Kennedy could ask Americans to go to the moon. We had the ability to develop the technology from our vast entrepreneurial culture and the wealth to back up the project.

Reagan could push the Soviet Empire to ruin because America had the economic muscle to build a military they could not match.

No longer is that economic muscle available. Now we ride into space on Russian rockets, and gave Putin Syria in the hopes he would resolve the mess Obama created.

According to progressives who work the halls of power, yet never built anything in their lives but political resumes, everything we have is government largess and direction.

Obama, who never had a real job, appears to have no clue how the vast social and economic ecology of the world works.

Governments can delegate resources for specific tasks but its primary function is to provide national security and universal law, allowing free creative energy to flow through the markets and into the world.

But our government now obstructs that flow and that has given us a decade of no-growth and put America in serious decline.

THE VAST WEALTH created by free enterprise and its ever-growing technologies has infused the radical progressives in government with the irrational idea of endless financial and technological surpluses to be used for their vision of the redistributive social justice society.

Rather than destroy capitalism, as some extreme 'degrowther' radicals demand, the current progressives simply want to use controlled capitalism as China is doing with its capitalist zones that create the wealth the government socialists need to stay rich and throw crumbs to the poor.

The allies of big government are crony corporate capitalists who use big government to their advantage. As the rich get richer, the once robust and growing middle class gets poorer.

When a country has 95 million of its citizens out of the work force, 50 million in poverty and 45 million on food stamps it's a new era. When the US taxpayers have spent over 22 trillion dollars on anti-poverty programs since Lyndon Johnson and poverty is worse, who benefited? Apparently, not the poor. The people who ran those programs and built careers on them benefited and still do.

THE PROGRESSIVE'S HOLY CRUSADE seeks to put the final nail in the coffin of the free market and bring production under the direction of the Superstate.

According to progressive illuminati Naomi Klein, one of the new breed of collectivist thinkers and author of *The Shock Doctrine: the Rise of Disaster*

Capitalism, the key to global peace and salvation of the planet is ending capitalism as we know it, and imposing the progressive, humanist control over the productive forces of the world.

Hugo Chavez, whose socialism destroyed Venezuela's economy, was one of her heroes. Unfortunately, Naomi wasn't available to hand out bread in the bread lines of that deteriorated nation in spite of having the greatest oil reserves in the world. Over a hundred years ago many academics believed that Venezuela would overtake the United States. Now that nation is on par with Cuba and other 'socialist' disasters.

Instead of Marx's dictatorship of the proletariat, we are now to embrace a dictatorship of the climate change master planners who insist they can rebuild the world's climate, even if they never built anything.

These progressive bureaucratic politicos just order their fantasies, pass ordinances, massive regulations and wait for the appearance of paradise. But their proven historic expertise is more about economic destruction than global reconstruction.

Reality suggests something radically different. That once societies move out of their third world poverty, become wealthy, population growth has a natural tendency to slow and technology has a natural tendency to grow, moving inexorably toward replacing the gluttony of a fossil fuel diet with cheaper and more efficient energies.

It is technological evolution, not leftist political revolution that matters for the future. And the more progressives retard what actually will end fossil fuel diets the longer it will take and the nastier it will become, socially and politically.

CHALLENGE AND RESPONSE in life and the field of battle for survival has had many contenders, but no response to humanity's poverty and misery and violence has equaled that of America's capitalism.

But, as that system is weakened from within, and faces global threats from without, our response may not be adequate to the challenges unless we experience a major course correction in the near future.

The West rose above all other cultures because it was forced, by trial and error, challenge and response, and a complicated, interconnected geography, to transcend the instinctive, universal, and historic hold of tribalism.

What began in the great empires, from Greece to Rome, then Europe and England, would create a new world with new forms of relationships: institutionalization of intelligence in universities, vast trade markets, banking and capital formation outside of the government.

When individuals operating in free market capitalism experiment, tinker, market, borrow and pay back, they grow wealthier by being rewarded by those who buy and benefit from their products. Markets release the intellectual potential of the human race. Great things follow.

THE WASHINGTON PROGRESSIVE ELITE demands the necessary power and wealth to achieve its great social goals. They see themselves as the true creative force, not those greedy entrepreneurs, tinkerers, and inventors. Government, they insist, must control the purpose, direct production and rule the entire life of society.

For the left to carry out its fantasies, individualism and freedom must be radically curbed.

There is a Dark Ages feel across our campuses and in the halls of power with the rise of the anti-capitalist mentality and the underlying call for the execution of the spirit of John Galt. There is no sharper sword to carry out that execution then massive, unsustainable debt.

Debt is a necessary byproduct of the progressive Superstate's ambitions, a necessary price to pay for reducing America's global hegemony and for saving the planet and creating help for the poor and social justice for all.

History suggests massive debt never helps the poor, but it does enrich the elite. It eventually debauches the currency and becomes the deathtrap of once great nations.

THIRTEEN

THE DEATHTRAP OF DEBT

Lenin was certainly right. There is no subtler, no surer means of overturning the existing basis of society than to debauch the currency. The process engages all the hidden forces of economic law on the side of destruction.

–J.M. Keynes, *Quoting Lenin*

AMERICA TOOK A STUNNING NOSE-DIVE from creditor to debtor in one of the fastest and largest financial reversals in history. We were the greatest creditor nation on the planet by 1980, before tumbling ignominiously down the slopes of financial madness to become the world's greatest debtor nation a generation later.

No other country on the planet owes as much as America's 20 trillion and counting, with unfunded future liabilities estimated to be 200 trillion by some economists and much higher by economic historian

Niall Ferguson who puts the number at 238 trillion.

Falling into massive debt eventually leads to currency destruction. It is the surest and shortest path to the suicide of a great nation. America is sliding fast down the mountain toward the financial cliff.

The long embittered Russians, having never fully recovered their self-esteem following the ignominious collapse of the Soviet Empire at the hands of Ronald Reagan, are joyfully watching our descent. They may not have all that long to wait. What sweet revenge. That will be the ultimate reset button.

When the superpower that protected the moral and physical base of civilization during and following WWII is no longer able, who will step in to confront Islamic supremacists, or Russian and Chinese expansion?

America, having lost its street cred around the world, will soon have little ability to change the course of events if it continues down this road to ruin. With the highest corporate taxes forcing an exodus of capital and manufacturing, where we're sending businesses to China and Mexico, and now even to Cuba, change is needed and needed soon.

Rumor has it that Michael Moore is upset that his prison-system vacation dreamland, Cuba, might be ruined by getting all capitalistic. And Hollywood actor Sean Penn is rumored to be equally aggrieved that his vacation paradise, impoverished socialist Venezuela, is turning in desperation to the great evil—capitalism.

But if Moore and Penn are patient their own country might become an impoverished paradise right under their feet and they won't have to go anywhere.

When the likes of a Mark Zuckerberg of Facebook gave up his American citizenship over the onerous taxes, he was just one of many. The superrich and big corporations can always find a way. But for the average American there is no escape from the crushing weight of debt and regulation in this brave new anti-capitalist world.

With the nation's belief in solvency dead and buried, America will become a nation by the government, for the government, and of the government and no longer controlled by the restraints imposed by a constitutional republic.

Isabel Paterson observed, "The true cause of Fascism, or Nazism, or Communism, is the structureless state, in which the whole energy of the nation, its production line, is thrown into the repressive mechanism of centralized government with status law. It is a deathtrap."

THE REVOLT COMING FROM MAIN STREET frightens the Washington establishment on both right and left. America's grassroots organizations are motivated and becoming angrier by the day at the collapse of freedom.

From the beginning we were a nation of

community action, whether raising barns, crossing the wilderness, creating schools, Little Leagues, or building community governments. In America there was a unique sense of ground level associations and local political action.

As Tocqueville observed, "Americans of all ages, all stations in life, and all types of disposition are forever forming associations." Some of those current associations are very angry and scary to the current establishments.

The progressive *wunderkinds* running the realm now look down from the great wall of the Beltway Camelot Castle and see a growing resistance.

What they are seeing is an awakening of America's fundamental, constitutional DNA that sees the rise of a collectivism that won't benefit the masses, but rather a tyrannical edifice built to control them as it enriches and empowers the plutocratic elites and enlarges the support base of dependents.

The primary goal of all ideological collectivists is to tear down the wall of separation of the citizen from the state, ferret out the rebellious contrarians and take them down one way or another.

Building the new social welfare state by endlessly printing money will eventually come to a nasty end. Unless, as happened at Plymouth Rock, there is a miraculous turnaround. But the defenders of the new order are many and the fight won't be easy.

Lenin also suggested that to carry out the grunt

work of building the new order on the wreckage of the old one needs the help of *useful idiots*. America appears to have no shortage of *useful idiots* across the campuses and in the halls of power.

While Lenin understood the mechanics of destruction of nations, he failed to understand how great nations were built in the first place. His communist collectivism led Russia down the bloody road to hell, filling the graveyard of the glorious dictatorship of the proletariat with tens of millions of victims.

THE MODERN TECH WORLD wasn't built in the East, or the Middle East, or Africa, or South America; it was the product of the West's response to its great challenges and spawned the Ages in philosophy, art, politics and economics unlike anything in the history of the human race.

The West emerged slowly and painfully through the endless challenges of war, disease, ideological and religious conflict over thousands of years. These heavily challenged societies escaped the iron grip of tribalism and responded to all these struggles by building the foundation for trade, science and inventiveness, from Greece to Rome, Europe and Great Britain.

These accomplishments would later reach fruition in America and create something unprecedented and unequaled in history.

But now that great human triumph is threatened by a new class of quasi-socialist welfare state bureaucrats. The political revolution that made America, that 'idea' of who we are as a unique ideology of freedom, is badly wounded and may not survive.

Freedom of thought, invention, and a place for it to come alive and prosper generated the rise of modern technology, creating energy ecologies unlike anything in history. These freedoms have tens of millions of feedback loops active 24/7 and are the lifeblood of the commercial society. But now that system is under serious attack.

Entrepreneurial capitalism is about something historically unique: the ability of regular folks to create wealth on open markets. That freedom is rapidly being closed by progressives who detest the essence of the American ideology. They are closer in spirit to Lenin and Trotsky, experts at destroying a culture, then Franklin and Jefferson, experts at building one.

DEBT IS THE DAMOCLES SWORD hanging over America's future. The endless appetite of the welfare state and its bureaucratization of society are creating an unprecedented dependency and corruption.

The welfare programs become such a powerful part of political culture they take on a metastatic dynamism that cannot easily be cut out. They seriously degrade the pulsating economic ecology of the marketplace upon which everything ultimately depends.

Legions of clueless bureaucrats have the powers to disrupt the flow of intelligence and response in the marketplace in the name of the salvation of the earth. What they do is create massive traffic jams, chaos and confusion. They stop the market from rewarding intelligence and instead reward futility, fantasy and massive failure. They create the conditions for a great nation to commit suicide.

Failure to understand this political and economic reality is like marching into a jungle deaf, dumb and blind. What awaits is not a loving embrace.

Weakened by unsustainable debt in a warp speed era filled with the weapons of mass destruction that are falling into the hands of pathological maniacs is a prescription for madness and national suicide.

FOURTEEN

TECHNOLOGY IN A MAD MAD WORLD

Technological progress is like an axe in the hands of a pathological criminal.

–Albert Einstein

MASS DESTRUCTION ORCHASTRATED by fanatics and psychopaths in the contemporary world is upon us everywhere. It may be our sad fate that we've opened ourselves up to becoming the victims of maniacs and death cults by our feckless foreign and domestic policies coupled with our technological brilliance.

The history of the evolution of speed is the history of a rising threat of predation. It took thousands of years, but warp speed has arrived.

Fanatic tribal cultures filled with envy of our success and anguish at their failure to innovate and invent, are stealing our technology with impunity to use against us.

Free societies and those in the grip of ancient totalitarian religious tribalism are on a collision course. In a warp speed world the battle will be very different from those in the past.

IN 6,000 BC CAMEL CARAVANS plodded across burning deserts in searing noonday sun. They were the fastest method of transport of goods and trade of that era, making an incredible eight miles an hour in a time when all of life, from trading to murderous, predatory raids, went at a slow pace that didn't change for thousands of years.

The fastest military force of the old era may well have been Genghis Khan's Mongol reign of conquest and terror until his death in 1227. His troops could make an incredible hundred miles in a day by constantly changing mounts, each soldier having up to four. The soldiers even learned to sleep on horseback while moving across the countryside.

Between Khan's romp and the seventeenth century when the mighty stagecoach rolled along at a speedy ten miles per hour the speed of travel and predation had not changed significantly.

Another great leap forward came in 1825 when the steam engine pushed speeds to an astounding thirteen miles per hour, allowing goods, travelers and armies to reach their goals at hitherto unimagined speed. But that was just the beginning.

In the following hundred years all hell broke loose. Airplanes could fly at over 100 miles an hour, unimaginable to early societies in their wildest fantasies. Killing became much easier and faster.

War technology, bombs, machine guns, and beyond, falling into the hands of the old politics pushed the world into a new, mass death phase and the new politics of ideological insanity with fascism and communism. The world found itself in major trouble.

In WWII, war planes reached well over 500 miles an hour to deliver their destruction and death. The world had changed and changed fast. But then a stunning shock—atomic bombs falling on Hiroshima and Nagasaki delivered by B-29 bombers obliterating those cities in fascist Imperial Japan. The warlords in that nation had no answer and surrendered.

In 1960 missiles snapped by at a nerve-racking 1,800 mph. The planet had been seriously, dangerously downsized. Warp speed now circles the globe and nothing is out of reach of mass destruction.

The omnipresent and instant speed of the internet and globe circling satellites brought about the world social media with its many benefits, but these technologies also presented the agents of darkness with new toys of recruitment in the pursuit of mass death.

Humanity faces itself in sideshow mirrors all over the globe in all its reptilian ugliness as death and destruction come fast and furious and everyone on the planet is vulnerable.

Obama's precipitous retreat from the Middle East helped unleash a new form of terrorism in ISIS that now has spread globally. Terrorists have created a university in Syria dedicated to developing sophisticated weapons for use in slaughtering Westerners around the world. Among their arsenal are chemical and biological weapons.

America, once upon a time the custodian of global sanity, is now in hiding from reality as our decline turned us from a lean, mean machine into an obese, bumbling bureaucratic State.

These gold-star progressive geniuses, many former 60s Maoists, now teach in schools and universities across the land and have lived in a fool's radical paradise their entire lives. They leave behind a critically weakened nation and a next generation of students unprepared to face the stresses that are awaiting them.

AMERICA'S DECLINE OPENS THE NATION to the globe's predators. And those predators are recruiting through social media and planning the death of the West while the Obama administration is busy seeking to destroy his real enemies, the populist, conservative opposition and 'outsider' rebels whose goal is to return government to its fundamental roots.

The anger of the opposition is based on a disturbing reality with a long list of problems and fears:

–A borderless nation

–Homeland Security employees on a terrorist watch list

–Intelligence agencies reports altered for Obama

–Serious criminals vanishing in sanctuary cities

–Green card visitors stay and vanish

–Absence of war strategy

–An economic recovery that wasn't

–Unsustainable debt

–VA disaster

–A Gyro chopper lands uninvited on the Capital lawn

–Drones cause airplanes to make avoidance maneuvers

–Terrorists use encryption to recruit

Newt Gingrich's observation about Obama being the greatest threat to national security to ever occupy the White House is being echoed across this stressed, angry nation.

The past is a blur, the future a lurking dystopian nightmare as this nation stumbles around in the dark while Obama works hard on his legacy, a legacy the millennials may not want to inherit.

THE RISE AND FALL OF NATIONS AND EMPIRES once took centuries, but now we are in the age of warp speed. Nations fall quickly and violently, as we've witnessed all over the Middle East.

The Roman Empire, winners of the wars of the Mediterranean, lasted somewhere in the vicinity of a thousand years, depending on start and end dates. The Ottoman Empire and the Spanish and English empires had half that shelf life.

The Nazi socialist warrior state envisioned its reign to be at least a thousand years, after killing and enslaving its enemies and grabbing resource rich lands, barely lasted a generation while triggering the global deaths of 50 million. And that number would be exceeded by the communists regimes murderous madness.

The Soviet Empire, considered by the ever enthusiastic, delusional Marxist intelligentsia of the day to be a political religion and the answer to all mankind's problems, the fulfillment of the inevitability of historic materialism, the archetype for the future of the entire world, didn't live up to the hype.

The unexpected collapse of communist Russia stunned the dedicated hard-core left intelligentsia around the world. They wept in shock, having believed all along it would be America that would fall, not the beautiful vision of the historical materialism under the aegis of the phony dictatorship of the proletariat.

In the Black Book of Communism, editor Stephane Courtois stated: "Communist regimes . . . turned mass crime into a full-blown system of government." The result was ninety-four million deaths under those regimes. But that was only the dead, not the hundreds of millions dislocated, and impoverished.

When the madness of communism tumbled ignominiously into the bloody graveyard of history, the left turned to another, more advanced tribal communal system, the grand Hegelian synthesis: crony capitalism under the rule of socialists in the post WWII era in pursuit of paradise.

The Obama administration, with the advice and consent of Hillary Clinton, sought to get rid of nasty dictators like Muammar Gaddafi in order to spread peace and tranquility to the Arab world. Obama seemed very enamored of Islamic culture and sought to bring a close relationship once dictators like Muammar Gaddafi were gone.

Unfortunately, on the corpses of old dictators comes chaos and opens the door even wider for the madness and spread of Islamic jihad.

Noble causes that rise from delusional, childlike thinking never have noble ends. And now that fanatics and mass murderers can get their hands on weapons of mass destruction we face a future that may be unlike anything we've so far seen.

THE AMERICAN PROGRESSIVE BLAMES all failures and miseries on rightwing conspiracies and Bush's wars, taking no responsibility for anything.

2010: the much heralded Arab Spring collapsed governments across the Middle East, leading to chaos to the dismay of the those who believed in the power of social media in the hands of the socially righteous who were cheering from their mother's basements, campuses and the Obama condos in the Washington beltway.

2011: Christian and sectarian genocide began in earnest and ISIS gets around nicely in the 2,300 armored Humvees we gave the disintegrating Iraq army.

2012: the vicious attack in Benghazi that killed the Ambassador and others and led to national humiliation and showed the Islamic terrorists that America was weak and, confused and had done nothing to protect those under assault. Then the administration tried to besmirch the brave men who fought to keep the people in the annex safe.

2015: the ignominious abandonment of Yemen with the marines leaving keys in the ignition of their vehicles and abandoned weapons as they ran to the waiting planes, some to end up dead in Afghanistan, a war that Obama promised to end and failed.

The pathological genie is out of the bottle and running wild. An unprepared civilization faces a modern technologically-fueled crisis. Overhead the Damocles Sword swings on a thread.

The sudden appearance of another holocaust raised its ugly head as North Korea tests intercontinental ballistic missiles, has nuclear bombs, and satellites with dangerous future capability.

The Iranian terror state builds centrifuges in preparation for becoming a nuclear power with Israel one of its prime targets.

As F.A. Hayek suggested, "It seems to be almost a law of human nature that it is easier for people to agree on a negative program—on the hatred of an enemy, on the envy of those better off—than on any positive task."

But for the obsessive, compulsive American progressives the enemy isn't *out there'*, it's always *'right here'* on the streets of fly-over America.

THE BATTLE IN AMERICA from Main Street to the universities and high schools, will ultimately be between the radical left and the insurgent right, between the neo-Marxists and the constitutionalists, between the welfare Superstate and the advocates of small government and free markets.

We are a radically factionalized nation at the worst of times. The traditional Republican and Democratic establishment politicians appear to be increasingly irrelevant to the major problems America faces.

Nevertheless, for the progressives, in spite of the crumbling world order, the big obsession is the looming crisis of losing power. Thus the obsession to build a massive dependent and dependable Superbase to ensure a progressive future.

Building the Superbase is the real goal behind open borders. It's not about altruistic compassion or the climate. It's all about a power base that will become so big that in the future it won't be challengeable.

FIFTEEN

BUILDING THE
PROGRESSIVE SUPERBASE

An "unemployed" existence is a worse negative of life than death itself. Because to live means to have something definite to do—a mission to fulfill—and in the measure in which we avoid setting our life to something, we make it empty.

–Ortega y Gasset, *The Revolt of the Masses*

MASS DEPENDENCY FOR THE PROGRESSIVE is the ultimate path to the creation of a permanent pool of 'post-proletariat' foot soldiers who will fulfill the progressive ambition for a de facto one party welfare Superstate run by the new secular priesthood.

As seminal economist L. von Mises, author of *'Human Action'* observed, "Every advocate of the Welfare State and of planning is a potential dictator."

The loss of both Congress and the Senate in Obama's second term drove the desperate progressives to get illegal immigrants into the voting booth by whatever means to prevent the ultimate horror, a rightwing 'outsider' winning the presidency and tearing down all their work.

The attempt by radical leftists to ridicule into oblivion conservative forces failed miserably. Instead, it helped promote a significant, angry backlash.

One of the key triggers in that growing anger came from the massive waves of illegal immigrants that Main Street saw as an attack on the very foundation of America.

Rational immigration was our legacy until *political immigration* emerged. If you opposed an open border and the cartels bringing up floods of illegal immigrants your 'racism', was showing. And if you show open reservations to Obama's disastrous foreign policy that has created the greatest refugee crisis since WWII, your 'Islamophobia' is showing.

Kate Brown, Democratic Oregon Governor, signed a bill to automatically register voters using data from the DMV, a move taken by other states like California to make it easy for illegal immigrants to get a driver's license and slip into the voting booth. These were big steps toward the goal of creating the Superbase.

Bringing on board the poor and distressed and hooking them up to the life-support system of government programs started with FDR, but is now in full swing to prevent the ultimate tragedy, the end of big government.

With 71% of every dollar the government takes in going to service debt and entitlements, speculation is that once we pass the $24 trillion debt level, added to the $200 trillion of unfunded liabilities, we are close to stepping off the cliff into a financial death spiral.

FUNDING THE WHEEL OF MISFORTUNE began with the relief for the destitute in the first food stamp program in 1939, following the total failure of the Roosevelt administration to solve the Great Depression.

The program was geared to the unemployed and farmers who were unable to sell crops. Food surpluses were made available and people paid for them with stamps. It was ended in 1943 when the global war against the Axis solved the unemployment and Great Depression problem.

In the post-Eisenhower era, when liberals came to full power, the food stamp program was resumed by JFK. His first Executive Order established the program as temporary and modeled on the depression era, but he displayed no desire to create permanent dependency on the state.

After Kennedy's assassination, the program was made permanent by LBJ. Enrollment skyrocketed from half a million in 1965 to double that ten years later, and tripled soon thereafter.

LBJ added new Great Society welfare programs and championed civil rights to help what he called his 'Nigras'. He and his successors would lock-in the black vote for the next sixty years giving democrats and later progressives 93% of the African/American vote.

But those Great Society programs over the long run helped destroy the inner city black family by making it easier to receive government largess than expand one's educational and economic potential. If a woman with children had no man in the house she was rewarded with financial largess from Uncle Sam, essentially making a father figure a liability.

Now we have 73% of black children born without a two parent family, where 1 in 3 black males in the inner cities will end up in some fashion registered in the criminal justice system.

The breakdown of the black family in the inner city and increasingly white families across the rest of the nation is a national catastrophe.

As Indiana Governor Mike Pence put it, "to those who say we should simply focus on fiscal issues, I say you would not be able to print enough money in a thousand years to pay for the government you would need if the traditional family collapses."

Black inner-city communities where the family has all but collapsed are now drug dealing war zones similar to some South American cities. An estimated $15 trillion has been poured into anti-poverty programs since LBJ. Where that money went once it funneled into these Democrat run cities with major ghettos is unknown. But poverty is worse now than when the Great Society programs began, proving Governor Pence's point.

JIMMY CARTER MADE FOOD STAMPS free in 1977. Then the stamps gave way to Electronic Benefit Transfer cards in 2002 during the Bush administration. And now SNAP, the supplemental nutrition assistance program.

Bill Clinton's 1996 'workfare' program, an attempt to get welfare recipients back into the workforce, was attacked relentlessly by democrats and finally undercut by an Obama edict in 2012. Mandatory work requirements were stricken from the program.

Progressives, with some help from establishment Republicans, are building one of the most massive entitlement and welfare programs in history.

The effort to create a dependent society ruled by elites will only happen if the resistant middle class is reduced and forced to seek help, and that is happening.

The disastrous reduction of the middle class to its lowest level in decades, falling below 50%, while the wealthy class working for the government has grown exponentially points to a new world in America. We are on the verge of creating a welfare tyranny.

Conservatives argue that poverty has never been overcome by anything other than strong families in an environment that protects the freedom of commercial activity, and gives individuals the right to own land, create businesses and have marketable skills, thus opening the way for gaining a sense of purpose and a path out of poverty. This is the environment being crushed.

For the progressives, the poor are far more than needy folks seeking help, they are a political necessity, a foundation on which great power emerges. Without the poor, progressive power is an empty dream, like a prince without peasants, a sheepherder without a flock.

In the Obama administration, the whole concept of 'work', once a religion in America, suddenly wasn't all that important.

BEING 'JOB-LOCKED' IS A CURSE declared Nancy Pelosi during her term as Democratic House leader. She basically articulated the widely held view on the left that low level 'work' is now obsolete in our high-tech society.

According to Pelosi, herself jobless her entire life, the social justice Superstate needs to free people from onerous low-wage jobs so they can pursue art, become poets, street musicians, surfer dudes, or Zen woodsy masterminds. And, of course, vote democratic.

People at the lower end of society are thus encouraged to give up any attempt to ascend through meaningless minimum wage jobs or pursue any advanced skillset, as it would take too long and wouldn't be a step up the ladder of success.

Given that we've sent most of our lucrative, middle-class manufacturing jobs overseas, allowing crony capitalists to bring in an unlimited supply of foreign green card holders, while illegal immigrants are busy picking our crops, building our houses, working in the food industry, and tending to our gardens, we now have over 95 million citizens out of the workforce. That figure will keep on growing given the policies we're following and the demographic of retiring Boomers on social security and Medicare. America is facing a national financial disaster.

One of the progressive's greatest success stories in America is the fall in income driving people onto the massive welfare state roles. Combined with the highest rise in food prices in our history, and employment at 62.5%, the lowest since 1978, meaning the real unemployment rate is much higher than the statistical fraud government is touting.

The stigma was not only removed from being unemployed, it was part of the new, high-tech world that no longer needed all that low level employment. Robots were taking over.

All we need, the progressive gold-star literati suggest, is that the techies work their sixty-hour weeks to produce enough wealth to take care of the post-work dude culture. With these tech folks producing the wealth, and progressives distributing it, peace and happiness, or at least progressive dominance, will be assured, and the progressive future secured.

The increasingly angry, populist Main Street insists that the true job-locked in America are establishment politicians who stay in Congress and the Senate for life and form nepotistic political dynasties.

Technological advances historically create more and more need for employees as every innovation spawns new goods and services and then spinoffs. Education has to constantly keep up with the changes.

But that's not happening in America's schools in this new age of the tyranny of good intentions. Now it's more about mastering politically correct thinking rather than employable skillsets. Besides, progressives argue, robots are taking over all low level jobs.

This vanishing job notion may well be just another Luddite moment in history. Robots need to be designed, manufactured, marketed, sold, delivered, and repaired. And who knows how many other new job skillsets will need to be created. Robotics may eliminate hundreds of thousands of old jobs, but create even more new technical ones.

The assumption that we already know the nature

and effect of the technological future ·is another example of the massive hubris of the intelligentsia of our time.

Ending self-reliance and building a massive base of dependents who expect all things from cradle-to-grave to drop from the loins of the nanny state is one of the major successes of progressivism.

But rarely has the deliberate destruction of independence been so nakedly celebrated as the monumental success of destroying Mountain Pride, a 'white' culture well outside the inner city. This was a historic textbook victory.

DESTROYING MOUNTAIN PRIDE became one of the most notable triumphs of the progressive agenda. While gaining greater and greater dependency in the inner city was easy enough, moving out into historically resistant 'white' mountain areas was very challenging and maybe not realistic.

As reported in the Chattanooga Times Free Press on July 11, 2012, the war conducted by the government against 'mountain pride' took place in the hardscrabble Appalachian Mountains in North Carolina.

The poor, who'd been there for centuries carving out their subsistence living, prided themselves on being self-reliant and strong, and refusing largesse from anyone, especially the federal government. They called their independent nature 'mountain pride', which, when translated meant: we may not have gold in our hills, or oil beneath our soil, but we will survive and do so without handouts.

Nothing so offends' the progressive mind as anyone claiming they aren't interested in government largess. To the true leftist any kind of real independence from the tribal community can't be permitted, so the recalcitrant 'mountain pride' folks, one of the toughest areas on the planet to recruit dependence, were targeted, harassed, bugged by persistent bureaucrats who'd been sent to end this nonsense and bring these resilient people onto the government welfare plantation.

Certain mountain folks were singled out and selected for continued pressure from the welfare recruiters. Finally, the weaker, more stressed, usually the females with children and no husband, were worn down. The stigma was removed. Food stamps were, after all, nutritional assistance for you and your hungry children. 'Mountain Pride's' historic resistance surrendered one SNAP (food stamp) recipient at a time.

It was a fantastic victory for the progressive interlopers. That victory was considered by the bureaucratic hierarchy to be so significant that banquets and bonuses went to the government agents in charge of defeating 'mountain pride'.

Never in the history of America had agents of the

government been rewarded for destroying the independence of a people for their own good. Indians were at least accorded the credit of being a defeated people and nobody thought it was for their own good.

But where will all of this lead when an 'unemployed existence' spreads from sea-to-shining-sea? Will the people wake up to the real cause of our problems, the crushing weight and cost of the Superstate's destructive and restrictive regulations?

Will the masses, with no mission, no purpose, bring forth beautiful art, fine music and brotherhood when no longer job-locked? Or do we face a future filled with flash mobs, orchestrated violence, and nihilism resembling an American Clockwork Orange?

SIXTEEN

AN AMERICAN
CLOCKWORK ORANGE

Go on, do me in, you bastard cowards, I don't want to live anyway, not in a stinking world like this one . . . It's a stinking world because it lets the young get on to the old like you done, and there's no law nor order no more . . .

–Anthony Burgess, *A Clockwork Orange*

WELFARE COLONIZATION of America's inner cities, and spreading across the land, cannot sustain a free country as we know it for long. But the progressive isn't interested in traditional freedom. Its agenda is about power and building a massive voting bloc necessary to create unchallengeable power.

The ramping up of race antagonisms, blaming 'white privilege', the war on cops, the explosive 'Ferguson effect' and the IRS assault, are all part of the divide-and-conquer strategy playing out across

America by the progressive left.

America's grievance industry, run by dedicated race hustlers, absolutely depends on a failed class of the poorly educated and unemployed. There's been a long tradition of a quid pro quo between victims of failed economic policies and those who wish to exploit that failure in the pursuit of expanding welfare dependency.

Neighborhoods in the city of Detroit, where 87,000 dilapidated and mostly empty homes are scheduled to be torn down, looks like something out of Ayn Rand's novel 'Atlas Shrugged'. According to ABC News, May 4, 2013, in Detroit's worst neighborhoods your chances of being a victim of crime are 1 in 7, the highest in the nation. LBJ's Great Society on meth.

But then there's bloody Chicago, a deeply corrupted city ruled by democrats since 1921, with its endless gun play, at times averaging five gang murders in a day, while the unions allow retired teachers to make double the average salary of Chicago workers. The relationship between big unions and democratic administrations has all but disenfranchised everyone else, especially the blacks in the ghetto who are treated like political slaves on the big government plantation.

NEO-MARXIST SAUL ALINSKY insisted that the radicals study the organization skills of Chicago gangster Al Capone to better learn how to attain and use power. They did as instructed and have exceeded Capone on almost every level.

As a result of rampant crime and corruption, Chicago went from the second most populated city to third and is heading downhill fast.

Obama's hometown is a war zone. In his two terms he has done absolutely nothing to alter that. His divisive rhetoric and failed policies have only exacerbated the problems.

For the violent schools in the inner city a solution was offered to deal with the attacks by students on teachers and each other. To counter this horror, Chicago's democratic mayor, and former Obama mentor, Rahm Emanuel, like his leftist touchy-feely buddy, socialist mayor of NYC, Bill de Blasio, initiated a *Restorative Justice Program,* using talking circles reminiscent of AA meetings.

In this stunningly bizarre form of pseudo social therapy, the victims must listen to the thug's grievances in order to help them find restoration. And, of course, none of that stop-and-frisk nonsense that old school Mayor Giuliani used to turn NYC from a crime den to a safe city.

Unlike crime waves of the past, there is something different emerging. Black Lives Matter, flash-mob uprisings, anti-wall street marches, are controlled by professional radicals, many financed by the likes of billionaire radical leftist George Soros. It is all about training of ground troops in its various political 'grievance' wars that might be the beginnings of a new fascism across our campuses in the name of political correctness and anti-capitalism.

IF CHALLENGE AND RESPONSE are the yin and the yang of a successful, fulfilling life, a life created in the context of strong families and communities, than a drug culture and welfare dependence are the opposite, leading to murderous punk gangs slaughtering each other in turf and drug wars.

What happens when the challenge is federalized and the response irrelevant? Good intentions infused with bad ideas driven by a sense of moral absolutism in politics have always created a hell on earth.

The ghetto young were turned into nihilistic, crippled fodder fed on hatred and lies and easy recruits as soldiers in the anarchist burn-baby-burn army.

One of the more disastrous government sociological innovations in the 60s and 70s, one that imprisoned many black communities, came from the construction of Soviet style housing projects for the poor in the inner cities, projects like Cabrini Green and the State Street Corridor in Chicago. Those projects became effective incubators of crime.

When the sons and daughters of Hollywood's elite back in the 60s triggered the drug trade, it would eventually hit the inner city like a slow motion dirty bomb in those Soviet style projects.

The inner cities have the highest murder rate, the least effective schools, inept or unconcerned teachers and the most broken families. Yet they have provided the democrats with a rock-solid 93% voting bloc in what may be the most successful political con game of all times, with residents getting nothing out of it but the rise of a 'thug' culture where education is a 'white' thing.

FROM PLANTATIONS TO THE PROJECTS TO PRISON was a widely used phrase among inner city blacks born in the womb of Soviet style housing in the drug infused projects of the inner city. What those communities needed, they were denied.

For blacks, robbed during slavery of their tribal African cultural heritage, kept in the darkness by illiteracy and ignorance for generations, then summarily dumped off in mass after the Civil War with no preparation to join in the entrepreneur process of American commercial success, faced one of the greatest struggles that any group has ever faced.

The response of the black communities had to be incredible, and with great determination they seemed poised to make a big move from athletic fields to Motown, from major writers and actors, black talents where obvious. But there was one arena that mattered above all in the long run, education and family as a base of preparation for business and the booming technology professions.

Rather than getting prepared for the future, inner city blacks were invited to be welfare dependents, and voters of course, a tragedy of epic proportions.

In a little acknowledged historic irony, more African blacks have immigrated to America since slavery than were brought over as slaves, and these immigrant Africans have an average income above whites.

The problem in the inner cities isn't about structural racism or 'white privilege', it's about lousy schools, broken families, and welfare dependency.

BLACK CONSERVATIVES RISING is a significant threat to the left. The emergence of young black intellectuals and political commentators are coming of age, taking the reins from old school rebels like Thomas Sowell and Condoleezza Rice.

According to this new wave of conservative black writers and bloggers like Crystal Wright (*Conservative Black Chick*) Dr. Ben Carson (*One Nation*), Jason Riley (*Please Stop Helping Us),* and Deneen Borelli (*Blacklash*), suggest it may be time to jettison 'The Good Ole' Government Plantation' run by race hustlers and race-card politicians. In full agreement is another very powerful, angry black voice, Sheriff of Milwaukee

County, David Clark, a voice of reason against the savage attacks on America's police.

Calling conservative blacks traitors, liars, Uncle Toms, and deserving of political death, is how progressives sought to destroy this feared enemy rising. Proving once again it's all about advancing progressive political power and has nothing to do with rebuilding the black family or advancing an education that will give young blacks a chance in the work world.

For an African American to walk off the progressive plantation, toss their race card into the trash can, and become both successful and conservative is a supreme and unforgiveable act of treason punishable by full-on character assassination.

AN AMERICAN CLOCKWORK ORANGE may be in our near future if the nation doesn't return to its inherent ideology of personal responsibility, education, family, community values and limited government because of:

–Massive drug abuse
–Disaffected and homeless vets
–Violent drug gangs like M13
–Mentally ill dumped on the streets
–Underemployment
–Radicalized college grads
–Professional anarchist street mobs

–Unsustainable debt and dependence

The British film '*A Clockwork Orange*' came out in 1971. If we fall into a nasty Clockwork Orange scenario, where no city street is safe, no program achieves its lofty goals, and fewer and fewer people find meaningful work, or a meaningful life, America will become that dystopian prophecy.

Take away challenge and response, struggle and consequence, values and civic virtues and you take away humanity and undermine civilization.

A storm is gathering and the American ship of state is listing, lost in the fog of this evolving crisis. If there is to be a great awakening in time to right the ship and change course out of the storm it will have come from the massive millennial generation.

If America isn't, as the millennials have been led to believe, the great evil of this world, but rather its salvation and sanity, then a massive rebellion is in order against what they've been taught.

If the American ship goes down it will pull down much of the civilized world with it.

The nation's historically largest generation is about to inherit a problem of enormous consequence for which they are ill prepared. They will have to make major decisions.

Gustave Le Bon, a controversial French social psychologist and anthropologist, observed it in his book in 1895—'*The Crowd: A Study of the Popular*

Mind'—that a person is only at their smartest when they are thinking alone, apart from the influences of family, friends and the din and pull of the crowd.

For millennials, breaking free of the mental straitjacket of the progressive politically correct mindset in order to see clearly what is at stake is an awakening that must happen if the course of this nation can be changed in time to prevent another great nation from committing suicide.

SEVENTEEN

THE MILLENNIAL
LION AWAKENS

*I don't know if you've ever been under ether. You come
out of it a little bit at a time. First a kind of gray light
shines on one part of your mind, just a dim gray light,
and then it gets bigger, but slow.*

–James M. Cain, *Double Indemnity*

SOMETHING UNEXPECTED AND DISTURBING
was going on in the streets outside millennial dorms,
apartments, and their parent's windows when the
young members of the largest American generation
began to emerge from a long political slumber to face
the distant wail of sirens, gunshots, and nightmarish
screams.

Their eyelids, heavy from the hangover after the
great celebration of hope-and-change, opened, not
with that jubilation they'd snuggled into their slumber

with, but by headaches and mounting angst at what was going on in the world. The tranquility and social justice they'd been led to believe would inexorably happen, never showed.

Strained eyes peeked apprehensively through the curtains of their protected youth into the dim grey light of an emerging reality so long ignored. Gone the music, the cheers, gone the joy of great expectations that held them as willing hostages. Having lived so long in a subjective 'feel good' state, the harsh reality of dawn appeared at first fragmented, like the last remnants of a serious binge.

As their new world slowly revealed itself, everything seemed wrong, contrary to what they had been promised, what they had embraced.

The rapture of Obama joy turned into a cold shock of uncertainty. Spring breaks and Apple releases, encryption battles not-with-standing, were still there, but the world they were about to inherit was in big trouble.

The millennials had believed Barack Obama was the leader who would bring social justice to America and peace to the world. He had seemed so perfect for the role, as if chosen by Hollywood casting as their savior from the horrors of the Bush and Cheney wars and the housing bust that triggered a major recession.

They'd been taught that the world's miseries were caused by American hegemony, that 9/11 was an act of understandable revenge by those we'd offended.

They'd expected Obama's pullout of the Middle East wars, and the reduction of American intrusions and the downsizing of the air force, army, and navy would change the hegemonic intrusion of America into the world's affairs. This in turn would necessarily lead to the goal of greater global tranquility.

But then a shocking, frightening glimpse of a mad world splashed through the gossamer curtains. It was a lot to see and accept. They hadn't inherited the peace and social justice they'd been promised, but rather a weakening, seriously divided nation in a world full of wolves: ISIS, the Paris and San Bernardino slaughter, Putin, China, North Korea, Iran, Syria's horror driving millions of refugees into Europe's multicultural embrace, Ebola, Zika virus, cyber-attacks, massive personal and national debt, the end of privacy and a broken border.

It was enough to make many young close those curtains to the world and try to go back to sleep.

THE STUNNED CHILDREN OF SOCIAL MEDIA were born into a world with an unprecedented plethora of entertainment options unknown in all history, and at a time of comparative ease, no scarcity of foods, and little struggle. These tech-spoiled, selfie millennials had advanced gadgets from smart phones to flat screen TVs, the internet and social media. They didn't have to train for war, just chill on self-fulfillment.

Wealth, it seemed for the first time in history, was nearly self-creating. They had little understanding of the hard realities of the past, the challenges and responses of pioneers in politics and technologies that created their world.

In college they could text and twitter, take lazy PC courses in feminism, Latino and black studies, absorb leftist sermons about identity politics from their liberal professors who assured them 'white' America was the cause of all the world's ills. It would be fixed by the new progressive superstars.

So now in the growing harshness of morning light, a big question arose like a mocking demon outside their windows. Was the 'Second Coming' really nothing but a big lie, a gigantic political con?

As the *kumbayah* 'we-are-the-world' joy slipped away, as the visions of the Promised Land went up in smoke and the beautiful music turned into the shrill clarion call of an uncertain trumpet. They felt betrayed.

Had their Boomer grandparents, those 60s radicals who had set this mess in motion and were now running around retirement villages in their golf carts, checking on their 401Ks, demanding raises in their social security, left their future generations saddled for life with crushing debt?

Anger replaced angst, rage replaced rapture. They began looking for someone to lead them to a better place. Someone other than the professional political liars they'd been listening to for so long. They wanted someone and something new. They needed to believe in a future.

THEIR LIBERAL CAMPUSES were overrun by PC thought police and fellow students demanding safe spaces free of mini-aggressions, while others demanded that the cafeteria provide authentic 'Third World' cuisine. Socialism had become very popular, a revolutionary change, even if nobody seemed to know what socialism really entailed beyond forcing the top 1% to pay off their school loans.

But something else was happening besides the rise of anti-free speech movements. The normal politically correct environment was being challenged from within by more conservative or libertarian students who were all constitutional and rebellious against what they saw as campus tyranny. Some joined rebel groups like Charlie Kirk's 'Turning Point USA', Evan Feinberg's 'Generation Opportunity', 'Operation Opt Out' or 'Young Americans Foundation', to name a few. It seemed that everyday some new Republican or conservative group was trespassing on their safe spaces.

This awakening of uncooperative millennial factions was far more disturbing to the progressive establishment and its supporters than the radio talk shows, the Wall Street editorial page, and evil Fox News with its cable dominance. Something had to be done to stop this anti-PC, potentially dangerous rebellion inside the universities.

The dominance of liberal thinking on campuses, accompanied by the blocking of conservative speakers and attempts to bring down their organizations with endless mockery of their ideas, was suddenly being challenged by students who still had some idea about the first amendment and the purpose of higher education and were willing to stand and fight back.

Like the country as a whole, the universities were experiencing a radical polarization.

A BIAS CLEANSE was demanded to counter this evil. It seemed like a stunningly brilliant way to bring the rebels back into the fold. It came from the stellar super-genius intelligentsia at MTV.

Millennials were informed that, contrary to their mistaken beliefs about themselves, i.e., that they were the first generation to be free of racism, sexism and other evils, they weren't free at all. They were harboring shameful, hidden racist ideas.

Proof came from an MTV poll which showed that 88% of millennials were opposed to affirmative action. The results showed millennials believed it did more harm than good if a minority had special privileges. Their legitimacy in the competitive world would be challenged and it wouldn't be in anyone's best interest.

That opinion alone was conclusive evidence that the millennials had still to be cured of their hidden evil beliefs. The solution was to demand they undergo a seven-day *bias cleanse* that would help these students recognize their evil hearts and secret racial prejudices and get them back on board the PC bus.

You have to be something of a mad political virtuoso to come up with a new way to guilt a generation that thinks of themselves as the socially most liberated in history.

For the progressives the real problem wasn't about race, it was that young rebels inside the universities were beginning to question the very core of the greater good of the new world order. They were counter-revolutionaries and had to be stopped.

Another major issue for the awakening millennials was the idea of their diminishment in the brave new world of their future, a world where they would no longer be significant as individuals, only as pawns in a world of progressive politics.

Millennials were told they needed to be 'fixed', that they were not free and clean individuals, but part of a collective problem. They needed not individual therapy, but group therapy. They were 'social' not 'individual' creatures. As such they had no absolute right to a personal, private life.

As Karl R. Popper related in, *'The Spell of Plato'*, ". . . a pawn, as a somewhat insignificant instrument in the general development of mankind."

THE END OF PRIVACY in the new tribal America demands there can be no really private persons. Privacy can't exist in a collective society. But that became something of an issue the millennials were forced to take seriously.

Big government, big corporations and foreign hackers spying into their lives, knowing their health care, finances, interests and desires, and the growing use of algorithms to predict future behavior, all part of this massive intrusion.

All those high-tech gadgets suddenly revealed the dark side when the government of Barack Obama funneled money into Homeland Security, the FBI and other agencies, tasked with investigating conservative and rightwing conspiracies, not potential Islamic terrorism.

That privacy can't exist in a tribal communal world was more than a bit off-putting. They began to take seriously a disturbing reflection of novelist and essayist Ayn Rand, "Civilization is the progress toward a society of privacy. The savage's whole existence is public, ruled by the laws of his tribe. Civilization is the process of setting man free from men."

The idea of the wonderful, hand-in-hand collective began to sound a bit Orwellian.

No argument in European history is as powerful and precise about this issue of individual privacy than between the English and the Germans. Oswald Spengler, a German philosopher of history, described the Germanic view, as opposed to the English view, that there could be, strictly speaking, "No private persons."

The millennials, educated to comply with altruistic social intent put forth by the progressive left, suddenly began to question what the *wunderkinds* were really up to with their uplifting narrative of redemption and renewal and the need to tear down traditional America to make way for the social justice Superstate.

Was the best political and economic architecture for civilization, that of collectivism or individualism? Did the Founders, those 'privileged whites' who were products of the Age of Reason, with teachers like Charles de Montesquieu, Francis Bacon, Descartes, and John Locke, actually know something?

Was constitutional America, in fact, the great exception to the misery and mistakes of history?

Stressed millennials found themselves in the center of a gathering political storm of major consequence, one that demanded either submission to the collective, or rebellion.

What they ultimately decide will determine

whether America remains the 'exception' to tribal collectivism in history, or just another great nation to fall on its own sword after having discarded all its principle core values.

EIGHTEEN

THE CENTER OF THE STORM

Woe for the house! Such storms of ill assail it.
My eyes are wells of tears and overrun,
And still I fear the evil that shall come.

–Euripides, *Hippolytus*

WHETHER THE CLASSIC AMERICAN 'IDEA' will survive, or has been irrevocably lost to the endless attacks from the left, depends on the outcome of the battle that is currently being waged on campuses, in coffee shops, across social media, and on Main Street.

The fundamental conflict facing America is whether its people are free to direct their own lives according to their personal beliefs and values in an open marketplace or whether they are nothing but cogs in the omniscient social justice Superstate?

MANY UNIVERSITY STUDENTS have engaged in a form of self-imposed mental repression and self-radicalization not unlike the process of a true socialist or jihadist as they submit to multicultural diversity and identity politics. They are not free individuals in a republic, but rather as true believers seeking this new identity in the collective. What the group thinks, they think. What the group does, they do.

Unless the radical leftist stranglehold on America's young minds is broken, and the 'exceptional' vision of a powerful, free people reestablished, the future will not be friendly, it will be violent, poor and broken. Paraphrasing Yeats, if the center cannot hold, surely we'll witness global anarchy loosed on our weakened and chaotic world.

The struggle threatening America's unique ideology has reached critical mass and engages every aspect of our culture, threatening to rip us apart in factional conflict even as the world order we have protected for over seventy years is on the verge of crumbling before our eyes. As Abraham Lincoln presciently stated during his speech at the 1858, Republican National Convention in Springfield, Illinois, "A house divided against itself cannot stand."

THE STUNNINGLY SUCCESSFUL ATTACK on America's core values has been in the making for a long time, with many parents. There is a growing sense that the elite progressive political culture, from the media to the White House and Hollywood, is completely invested in a delusional, dangerous mirage that coalesced out of the radical political muck of Chicago. Their ambition, once in power, was to rend asunder old, overly white, hegemonic America and build a tribal wonderland on the wreckage.

When Obama came to power he had both houses and full command of the liberal media, the progressive literati, and Hollywood. It was full steam ahead to finish what the 60s radicals had started.

It was assumed by the dedicated, teary-eyed devotees that Obama and his entourage knew how to rule, how to legislate, how to calm the world.

Beyond the glowing rhetoric and great feelings, that anticipated tranquility was run over by ISIS pickup trucks filled with madmen preaching Armageddon and waving the black flag of death.

Obama's real ambition was always his campaign against traditional, conservative America. His main tactic from the beginning was Alinsky's divide and conquer. He never really tried to hide his intention to bring America down to the level of lesser nations.

Yet many people outside his hardcore supporters refused to believe this wildly celebrated first African/American president actually meant what he said.

Obama's real legacy is his success in weakening and factionalizing America. But the unintended consequences are not what his delusional thinking anticipated. A weak America didn't lead to tranquility and peace in the world. Instead it led to chaos and global terror as the predators around the globe are loosed on a world that has lost its center.

THE SUICIDE OF GREAT NATIONS always involves massive debt, pervasive corruption, a declining economy, and delusional visions.

Whether the historic American political DNA can bring about a reversal of course is yet to be clear. Those who demand a return to constitutional 'negative' governance versus those who believe in an even more massive 'positive' rule are both in a rebellious mood, both seeking to take the White House and change the nation's course.

This anti-establishment insurgency that is gathering for all-out political battle across the nation is just the beginning of what the future will bring. It is a potential conflict scenario between extremes that may remain within the confines of the laws and rules of the republic, or, if major events destabilize the country further, we may face violence in the streets and the potential for serious civil strife.

Will Madison's alarm that factionalism will tear us down be proven? Is our demise, as Lincoln feared, going to come from within?

The great struggle of our time, personal and

constitutional, is not between traditional Democrats and Republicans. It is between the idea of freedom versus the idea of a tribal collectivism, between the individual and the communal, between the ideas of a free society against the vision of a social justice society run by plutocrats who, while amassing fortune and fame, destroy the foundation of a great nation.

THE BATTLE LINES ARE DRAWN as Americans face the ultimate struggle. We are either a free people, a nation of self-reliant doers, inventors and tinkerers in control of our own lives and destinies, accepting our failures and successes, or we are destined to be restructured by bureaucratic superstars who spend their days talking and thinking great thoughts, and aspire to build vast political empires on illusionary foundations.

America has fought off the concept of collectivist 'positive' power its entire history and the results have been unequaled. The superiority of America lay in the thinking of the Founding Fathers that led to the Constitutional separation of powers, the Bill of Rights and a new political ideology. America is the product of the architecture of 'negative governance' built by the Golden Age of political thought.

The transition from small farmers and pioneers to big city factory workers, from horse and wagons to cars and airplanes, from wood fires and gas lamps to electrifying the world, from telegraphy to computers and on to the moon are the products of the energy and genius of a free society.

If a reversal of course such that happened with the pilgrims in 1623, under religious leader, William Bradford, does not take place soon, humanity will lose the greatest social and economic experiment and protector of freedom the world has ever known.

This nation is on the razor's edge. If the wrong choices are made, if America's constitutional republic becomes another great nation to fall on its sword, our doom will bring the world into a violent, tribal Dark Age filled with weapons of mass destruction and ideologies willing to use them without restraint or remorse.

Such storms of ill assail us!

It is in America's DNA to rise up and fight to regain her freedom and reignite the torch of liberty, that is, and always has been, our manifest destiny.

—THE END—

ABOUT THE AUTHOR

RICHTER WATKINS is an essayist and bestselling thriller writer. He's a Vietnam veteran, former boxer, martial artist, and pistol champion. He earned an MFA from the American Film Institute and a degree in sociology from San Jose State. His essay on 'Deliverance,' under his pen name 'Terry Watkins,' can be found in THRILLERS: 100 Must Reads.

You can reach Richter at: www.richterwatkins.com
Facebook: www.facebook.com/richterwatkins
Twitter: @richterwatkins

OTHER WORKS
BY RICHTER WATKINS

The Murder Option 1, 2, 3
The Girl On The Golden Elephant
Operation Chaos
Cool Heat
Betting On Death

WRITING UNDER TERRY WATKINS

The Big Burn
Stacked Deck

SOURCES

Alinsky, Saul. *Rules for Radicals,* 1961.

Aurelius, Marcus. Roman Emperor 161-180 AD. *Meditations.*

Beinart, Peter. *The Crisis of Zionism.*

Bradford, William. *Of Plymouth Plantation.*

Burgess, Anthony. *A Clockwork Orange.*

Cain, James M. *Double Indemnity.*

Chomsky, Noam. linguist, philosopher, anarcho-syndicalists, leftist leader and self-proclaimed libertarian socialist.

Courtoes, Stephane. *The Black Book of Communism, 1997.*

D'Souza, Dinesh. *Obama's America-Unmaking the American Dream, 2012 Regnery Publishing, 2012 Threshold Editions.*

Einstein, Albert. *The World as I see it, 2006,* Kindle Edition, Ideas and Opinions, 2010.

Emanuel, Rahm. Obama's White House Chief of Staff in February, 2009 about the value of using crisis.

Euripides. *Hippolytus*. Greek tragedy in 428 B.C.

Ferguson, Naill. *The Ascent of Money, a Financial History of the World*. The Penguin Press, 2008.

Figueres, Christiana. The executive of the UN Framework Convention on Climate Change, May 17, 2010. Supporter of China's one party state as best answer to climate change policy.

French, David. Contributor to Jay Sekulow's *Rise of ISIS: A Threat We can't Ignore*. Howard Books, October 14, 2014.

Gingrich, Newt. *50th Speaker of the House of Representatives 1995-1999. Conservative spokesman, major critic of Obama.*

Gasset, Jose Ortega Y. *The Revolt of the Masses. W. W. Norton & Company, 1932.*

Gruber, Jonathan. MIT professor of economics and one of the architects of Obamacare.

Hayek, F.A. *The Road to Serfdom. Originally published in 1944. Powerful argument against collectivism.*

Hegel, Georg F. W. *The Dialectics of History.*

Hitler, Adolf. *1927 Nuremberg Rally speech*. Translated by Randall Bytwerk.

Hoffer, Eric. *The Ture Believer.* Harper and Brothers, 1951.

Hofstadter, Richard. *Historian, Age of Reform. Knoff 1955. Anti-intellectualism in American Thought. Knoff 1963.*

Jefferson, Thomas. Our 3rd president and a Founding Father and principle author of *the Declaration of Independence.*

Kant, Immanuel. German philosopher (1724-1804), author of *The Critique of Pure Reason.*

Kerry, John. Secretary of State.

Keynes, J.M. Quoting Lenin.

Kilmeade, Brian. *Thomas Jefferson and The Tripoli Pirates-The Forgotten War that Changed American History.*

Klein, Naomi. *The Shock Doctrine: The Rise of Disaster Capitalism.* June 2008, Metropolitan Books.

Lamm, Richard D. 38th Governor of Colorado. February 09, 2008, speech at Federation for American Immigration Reform.

Lewis, C.S. British novelist, Medieval and Renaissance scholar. *The Chronicles of Narnia.*

Lincoln, Abraham. 16th President. *Emancipation proclamation* (1863).

Lord Acton. (1834-1902). *Selected Writings of Lord Action* by John E.E.D. Action.

Lynch, Loretta. Attorney General under Barack Obama.

Madison, James. The 4th President and one of the principle Fathers of the Constitution.

Mises, L. von. *Human Action, A Treatise on Economics.*

Montesquieu, Baron de. *The Spirit of the Laws.*

Murray, Charles, *American Exceptionalism.*

Orwell, George. *Animal Farm.*

Paltrow, Gwyneth. *Advising Obama about Power at a Hollywood party.*

Paterson, Isabel. *The God of the Machine.* The Caxton Printers, Ltd. Caldwell, Idaho 1964, Copyright 1943.

Pelosi, Nancy. House Speaker who declared in March, 2010 about Obamacare, *"We have to pass the bill so you can find out what's in it."*

Pence, Mike. *The 50th Governor of Indiana on the breakdown of the family.*

Popper, Karl R. *The spell of Plato*

Rand, Ayn. *The Romantic Manifesto, A philosophy of Literature.* New American Library, 1971, *Capitalism: The Unknown Ideal,* A Signet Book, 1967.

Reagan, Ronald. August 06, 2011 speech.

Roberts, John. Deciding vote on Supreme Court in 2012 to save Obamacare.

Socrates. *Plato's Republic.*

Spengler, Oswald. *The Decline of the West.* (1918).

Steyn, Mark. *After America.*

Sophocles. *Antigone, The lament of Teirsais.*

Tocqueville, Alexis de. *Democracy in America.* Anchor Books edition, 1969.

Turley, Johnathan. Legal scholar, professor at George Washington University.

Yeats, W.B. *The Second Coming.*

39896027R00095

Made in the USA
Middletown, DE
21 March 2019